Why I will ALWAYS be vegan

125 essays

from around the world

Compiled

by

Butterflies Katz

This book serves as a public statement dedicated to the clarification and the preservation of what it means to be vegan.

With much appreciation to vegans worldwide, especially isolated vegans, and those who submitted an essay that was selected for this collection. Much gratitude to Angela Radich, without whom you would not be holding this book in your hands. Thank-you Rolanda from Evolve Campaigns - U.K., for the front cover and all you do, and to Chelsea Dub for the artistic back cover. Thank-you to everyone who contributed photos or artwork for this book. All the photos provided by and of Karrel Christopher displaying beautiful interspecies connections are even more impressive knowing that the animals are farmed animals she has befriended in her neighborhood, not animals in a sanctuary. Finally, a big heartfelt thank-you to Gentle World for hours of editing help, and for the wonderful life I live!

~ M 'Butterflies' Katz

www.thevegantruth.blogspot.com

Photo by Hof Butenland farmed animal sanctuary, Germany

LIST OF ESSAYS

Photo by El Hogar ProVegan animal sanctuary, Spain - www.elhogarprovegan.org

Introduction

Over the years, many vegans and animal rights advocates have been saddened to watch the concept of veganism become misappropriated. Although the term is now much more widely known, it has come to mean different things to different people. The definition of this powerful and profound word has been assimilated into the general public's vocabulary often diluted and even devoid of its meaning.

For clarity we cannot turn to dictionaries or other non-vegan sources to understand and define veganism, but we can look instead to vegans themselves and vegan organizations. The founding members of the first vegan society (formed by Donald Watson in the United Kingdom in 1944) initially only defined the vegan diet. In 1949, one of the founding members, Leslie Cross, pointed out that the society lacked a definition of veganism and he suggested the following: "The principle of the emancipation of animals from exploitation by man." This was later clarified as: "To seek an end to the use of animals by man for food, commodities, work, hunting, vivisection, and by all other uses involving exploitation of animal life by man." The actual definition of "veganism" set forth in 1979 by The Vegan Society is as follows:

> A philosophy and way of living which seeks to exclude—as far as is possible and practicable—all forms of exploitation of, and cruelty to, animals for food, clothing or any other purpose; and by extension, promotes the development and use of animal-free alternatives for the benefit of humans, animals and the environment.

In 2011, I conducted a survey online that was responded to by 850 vegan activists, who voted for the following definition of veganism:

> Recognizing the right of all sentient animals to be treated with respect and justice, vegans do not consume, wear, or use animals or take part in activities of their exploitation, as far as reasonably possible.

After a recent increase in public declarations from individuals calling themselves "ex-vegan", the need became apparent for a campaign that would illustrate the fundamental flaw in such a label, and to draw attention to the real meaning of the word "vegan".

To raise awareness of the philosophical reasons why one becomes and stays vegan, I held a short essay contest asking participants to tell me "why they will always be vegan". People of all ages from around the world stepped up to share their points of view. After the competition, in order to further empower this collection, I added more essays contributed by authors from all continents.

It was an unexpected pleasure to see that those who have a deep understanding of the vegan ideal emerged from every corner of the globe, demonstrating that the commitment to being vegan is a phenomenon taking root from Portland to Poland, from Hollywood to Hawaii, and even in countries with economies largely based on animal exploitation.

This expanding reach of the vegan way of life confirms that our collective consciousness is waking up to the fact that veganism is a Great Truth; a philosophy that is beneficial for the whole, inclusive of the entire planet and all its inhabitants, and a hope for our future.

Arranged in random order, the following short essays offer valuable insight into the perception of a committed vegan. Now English-speaking readers everywhere have the opportunity to be touched by these heartfelt, honest, soulful, clarifying, and compelling words.

~ M 'Butterflies' Katz

July 2015

Photo by C-A-L-F Sanctuary, United Kingdom

2

Keith Berger, South Florida, USA

I will always live vegan because, ever since the moment my eyes were opened to the horrors and atrocities of the culture of animal exploitation pervasive throughout our current global community, I refuse to participate in, support or encourage the system of animal slavery, torture, rape, mutilation, deprivation and wholly unnecessary and unjustifiable death I see all around me.

Humans do not kill and eat animals for necessity, though that is the myth to which many cling. Rather, humans slaughter billions of land and sea animals each year for habit, tradition, convenience and taste, none of which would hold up in court as worthy defenses were we to use these as justifications for having killed even one human animal.

The moment I realized the animal holocaust of which I had been a participant, a light turned on inside me that cannot be turned off. I immediately understood that since I would not knowingly support the terrorism, bullying, rape, and murder of members of my own species, I also couldn't justify condoning such behavior across species. As one person elegantly put it, when my heart spoke louder than my stomach, I changed forever.

Because it was the normal, accepted way of raising a child in the United States (today I know "normal" is just a setting on a washing machine), I was forced to consume products of animal exploitation and indoctrinated into an animal-product addicted culture before I was able to make my own choices. Once I knew the truth and learned I had other choices, I made the compassionate choice to live a vegan lifestyle.

A plant-based diet is far healthier for humans and the planet than one involving the raising and killing of non-human animals for food. As any of the millions of vegans— and non-vegans—around the world know, consuming products of animal exploitation is unnecessary, gluttonous and cruel, as well as wasteful and environmentally damaging. It comes as no surprise that a way of life linked to such internal maladies as cancer, heart disease, impotence and diabetes would also have adverse effects on our external environment.

I will always live vegan because I am no longer selfish enough to require that another sentient being should suffer and die for my convenience. I live for the day we no longer have to create humane societies, but instead simply choose to live as one.

Achim Stößer, Germany

Founder of *Maqi - for Animal Rights, against Speciesism*

Veganism is not about our health but theirs; it is about ethics, not food; about animal rights, not cupcakes.

Since I became vegan I have seen many more animals suffer and die than ever before, not in videos or in photographs, but in reality. I have seen thousands and thousands of chickens, cows, geese, pigs, and turkeys imprisoned to gain anything, from their glandular secretions to their very own corpses, for consumption. Many of them already dead, were lying among their kin or in trash bins, the others doomed to be murdered. Yet I was not able to free more than a few dozen birds (mostly hens) and even fewer mammals—a raccoon from a box in an allotment garden, a cat who lived in a birdcage, a horse one day before he would have been sent to the slaughterhouse, dogs, foxes, guinea pigs, minks, rabbits, and sheep. Speciesists who regard animals as property call it larceny.

What impacted me most was a cow who was killed before my very eyes when I had only been vegan for three years, and just had started my abolitionist activism which led me to an abattoir. This traumatic event made sure that, unless I will be subjected to a lobotomy or my brain will be sipped by alien brain suckers or munched by zombies, I will always be vegan.

To replace the captive bolt gun, the slaughterhouse managing director (who happened to be the supervising veterinarian of the slaughterhouse and an animal welfarist), tried to introduce a new "animal friendly" electric stunner. They used it on several sheep, a bull, and two cows. Now this cow was hanging, from a chain tied around her hind limb, seemingly unconscious. A stream of blood as thick as my wrist splattered from her throat. Then she regained consciousness. She opened her eyes, opened them wide in fear and pain. Standing a few feet away at her side I looked into her left eye while she looked into mine. She raised her head for a moment and the fountain from her throat grew even thicker. It seemed like she tried to scream; a silent scream from someone whose throat was cut, which led to a death rattle. There was nothing I could do to help her. That was some twenty years ago, but these images are burned into my brain; I will never forget that glance she darted at me.

Angel Flinn, Hawaii, USA

It's been nearly 14 years since I had my vegan epiphany and vowed to never again partake of, or participate in, anything offered by the machine of violence that we call the animal industry. Since that time, my understanding of veganism has continued to grow and deepen, until it has become such an integral part of my ethics and my values that I can no longer imagine being able to separate from it, and still be able to look at myself in the mirror with a clear conscience.

To no longer be vegan would mean to deny the most obvious truth I have ever learned, and to turn my back on every single animal who is counting on me and others like me to advocate for them in a world where they are seen as disposable objects rather than sentient individuals.

To no longer be vegan would mean to pretend that I do not know what is really going on—on the farms, in the hatcheries, in the slaughterhouses, in the laboratories, in the oceans, and everywhere else on this planet where animals are treated as resources for us to exploit.

To no longer be vegan would mean to deny my true nature as a person who can feel for the pain of others, and who aspires to live as peacefully as she can in this far from peaceful world.

To no longer be vegan would mean to return to a world of darkness, for it would require me to close my eyes to the light of moral progress that illuminates the way forward to a better world for us all.

But perhaps an even more saddening thought is that it would require me to extinguish the light of my own integrity, which is the source of my faith in myself, and which I count on to show me my own next steps on my way to a better self.

Angel and rescued rabbit Poof, Gentle World

Rhonda Anderson, Alberta, Canada

I will always be vegan because of the simple fact that each and every individual who can experience suffering and joy, and who would continue to live out their natural lifespan if left to do so, possesses the right to live free from oppression, and this right deserves respect. If this right is not respected, where is the line of basic respect drawn for anyone? What then would constitute having the right to be respected? Where sentient individuals are concerned, I see that injustice to some of us ensures injustice to others of us. For the sake of all, there needs to be justice for all.

Upon discussions about veganism, I've had a member of my family tell me I'm selfish to think that they ought to be vegan too and a friend tell me I only want them to be vegan for the sake of having my way. My being vegan is the furthest from being selfish that I can be, because it involves the recognition that I am that family member, and I am that friend, and I am every being experiencing oppression or respect, and each of them is me. When it comes to being oppressed or respected, we are all equal. To me, to include and consider the well-being of those animals who are not human is part of considering the well-being of anyone and everyone since, essentially, we are all the same. If I were to witness my aforementioned family member or friend being mistreated and I decided to stand up for them, to acknowledge the injustice that was being done to them, to decide to not be complicit in the lack of regard shown to them and to expect others to do the same, would I be viewed as selfish and as only wanting things to be my way? No, I would not. This is why I will always be vegan.

All of us, no matter our perceived differences, share what matters, and what matters is sentience. We, all of us human and non-human animals alike, feel. Having sentience is the basic criteria for being allowed to live free from oppression, and our right to not be oppressed must be respected. To respect means to be vegan.

Photo provided by Karrel Christopher - www.karrelchristopher.com

Emmy James, Waikato, New Zealand

One day in March 2007, when I was 13 years old, I decided to go vegan. Simply because I knew it was the right thing to do. Why should I participate in horrible violence towards other animals when there was absolutely no necessity to do so? It just didn't make sense to me. So, overnight, I became a vegan and stopped participating in animal use for food, clothing, testing, entertainment and any other purpose. Seven-and-a-half years later, I am still vegan. And I can say with absolute certainty that I will always be vegan. Because it isn't about me.

Veganism is the recognition that other animals are sentient individuals, just as we are, who deserve to live their lives free from enslavement and exploitation. They are the victims of our non-vegan choices. And when there are victims involved, a choice is not personal. It is not something as simple as choosing what music to listen to or what colour t-shirt to wear. Whether we want to believe it or not, the simple fact is when we purchase non-vegan products, we are actively participating in the harming and killing of others.

How could I ever go back to that? To deciding that the small, personal benefits I might get out of using animals is more important than their lives? I have seen the fear they feel when they are about to be killed. I have watched them struggle and fight for their lives. I used to disregard that suffering and push my feelings away. To do what everyone else was doing. But I refuse to do that anymore. Using non-human animals may be the norm, but that does not make it right. Those lives matter. They are not ours to use and do whatever we like with. I will always be vegan. It is who I am. It is not a diet. It is not a lifestyle. It is a stand for justice.

Photo by El Hogar ProVegan animal sanctuary, Spain - www.elhogarprovegan.org

Lisa Qualls, Reston, Virginia, USA

It is simple, really—once you respect the rights of others, how do you stop respecting them? Just like almost everyone else, my potential for compassion was hobbled at a young age. I grew up on a mountain, around hunting, and went to school with farm kids. I saw the victims on farms in herds and flocks, their individuality ignored. I even personally murdered some animals. I have a lot to feel guilty about.

It was not until I met my husband, Shelby, that I started to understand compassion for those who are not human. Shelby's experience with other-than-human persons growing up was more compassionate than mine, and his knowledge of them through reading was extensive. Listening to him I learned so much about the sentience and majesty of other animals, and I grew to respect them a little. It took a bumper sticker to jolt us: "If you love animals, why do you eat them?" It took us three months to stop eating their flesh and wearing their skins. Over the next three years, I learned a lot of details of all forms of animal exploitation and other avoidable harms. I became an activist, unlearned speciesism, and I finally became vegan. I did it so gradually, thinking the entire time that I could not do it, that I don't even know for sure when I was vegan, but I have decided it was the fall of 2004.

Unlearning speciesism is the foundation of veganism, connecting one with the world in an amazing and complex way. I now know that everyone has an equal right to live free from exploitation and other avoidable harms, including a right to their share of a healthy planet. How could I ever feel differently?

Photo by El Hogar ProVegan animal sanctuary, Spain - www.elhogarprovegan.org

8

Sun, Hawaii, USA

Co-Founder of *Gentle World*

In the heat of the summer of 1966, revolution was in the air. Black people were revolting against the injustice of whites, women against the domination of men, and young people everywhere were expanding their minds beyond the restrictive perceptions imposed upon them by their parents, teachers and governments. Like a hurricane, the winds of change swept through the world, blowing away centuries-old dogma, and leaving in their wake a higher consciousness than had ever been known before.

It was during that summer that Light and I forged the bond that has held us together through all the years since. In the spirit of the time, we took a vow to ourselves, each other and whomever else was listening, to pursue not the lies we saw being exposed all around us, but the absolute truths that we had been told didn't exist. We vowed to discover those truths and to hold each other to the task of living them.

Our test came soon after, when we saw a movie in which was depicted the slaughter of a bull. Three men were standing in hip boots, ankle deep in blood. They were all hitting the bull on his head with sledgehammers, but the huge animal did not die with one blow. He screamed louder and louder each time, until he fell to his agonizing death at the men's feet. I will never forget those screams as long as I live.

We walked out of the theatre horrified but resolute in our decision to never eat another animal again. Over the next few years, as we learned that no animal product (whether for food, clothing or anything else) could be produced without some form of cruelty and violence, we veganized our lives, without yet knowing the word.

Because it embodies the values we had always believed in, such as justice, kindness, gentleness and compassion, veganism became the foundation of our higher selves. In its light, we were able to recognize and evolve aspects of our behavior that were inhibiting the growth of our noble nature, and to eliminate them, one step at a time. If we were to forsake the vegan ideal, that foundation would crumble, toppling our higher selves, along with our cherished values, until there was nothing left of us of any value. Perish the thought.

Light, Hawaii, USA

Co-Founder of *Gentle World*

This is the first irrefutable truth I discovered in my life; that eating and using animals is, no matter how you look at it, an act of abject cruelty. When we eat or use animals, we are hiring the butcher or dairyman or furrier to kill or abuse the animal for us. We are, in effect, guilty of murder for hire.

I became aware of this fact personally when I witnessed the slaughter, by sledgehammer, of a screaming bull. I felt at the time as a German citizen might have felt in 1943, had he suddenly become aware of The Holocaust. Imagine what a life-changing awakening that was for the German and for me! We both discovered we were living a lie; the lie being, in each case, that there was no holocaust going on.

My soul made a promise to that bull and to all animals. I gave my word that I would do all I could to end the horrific human treatment of animals. My first course of action was to stop my own eating and using of them. I later learned that the path of Ahimsa or harmlessness I had embarked upon was named VEGAN.

I made that promise 44 years ago. I will never go back on my veganism or my word. I trust that, by now, the animals know that they can count on me.

Light and Braveheart; a forest deer

Roger Yates, Ireland

When I was a kid, I had a strong sense of fairness. I would judge things in terms of whether it was fair or not. I always extended that principle to other animals. As a teenager, I was found jumping from desk to desk to let wasps out of school windows while everyone else was trying to kill them.

As a young projectionist in his first job, I witnessed an usher killing a crane fly with her shoe because she felt the insect was "ugly". I thought she was pretty ugly but I would not think it fair to attack her with a shoe.

In 1977, I became interested in anti-bloodsports. By 1979 I was a fully-fledged hunt saboteur but also a vegan for ethical reasons. One push towards veganism was a TV news show which featured seal killers in Scotland complaining that the seals were eating "their fish". I reasoned that the seals had simply got to the fishes before the humans had. Killing seals for that reason didn't seem fair.

Of course, once I learned about every other aspect of animal use, my commitment to veganism was complete. Looking back, I'm extremely grateful that I never went through a period of being a vegetarian. Vegetarianism, I agreed with Donald Watson, is an ethical half-way house and not for me. I don't think it's fair to steal eggs from birds and calf food from calves.

I now understand and appreciate the holistic, expansive, vision of veganism held by the pioneers in the 1940s and 1950s: that veganism is part of the peace movement and looks towards the moral evolution of humanity. It is now the guiding philosophy of my work for the rights of human animals and non-human animals. Will I be vegan for the rest of my life? You bet your cotton socks I will.

Photo by Hof Butenland farmed animal sanctuary, Germany

Jan Claus Di Blasio, Rome, Italy

True human goodness, in all its purity and freedom, can come to the fore only when its recipient has no power. Mankind's true moral test, its fundamental test (which is deeply buried from view), consists of its attitude towards those who are at its mercy: animals.

Milan Kundera, 'The Unbearable Lightness of Being'

Have you ever looked into the eyes of a sow? Do you truly think that we lack the means to communicate across species? She is not the "mere animal" you think you know. She senses and smells your presence. She can see your silhouette cast against the light. She advances, timidly, and seeks your eyes. Her orbs measure you, depose your shield of solid convictions and seek the empathic spark that is dormant within you. Indifference ceases where eyes meet: we are drawn to the deep moonlit wells of the other, burrowing deep in the psyche as we disturb the murky waters of ourselves. This introspection, this deep instinctive soul-searching is the galvanising spark that tears off the blindfold of our self-centred existence as we can lie to ourselves about the other, but we cannot do so without betraying the feral emotions that surge within us. It reminds us that, on this precious planet, we share our paths with other beings; beings gifted with the primeval urge to pursue an existence free from pain and humiliation.

To some, veganism may just be a label, a passing fad, a radical extremist statement against sensible norms; to others, common earthlings like ourselves, it is the promise of social justice made to the eyes of the sow and to many others. It is an oath, a pledge to recognise that all eyes are a window to a sentient being but also mirrors reflecting back the suffering that we, as a society, inflict on the defenceless. I have looked into her eyes. I have not seen the raw mechanics of Descartes' automata. I have not seen the acquiescent victim of the Dominion contract. I have seen dread, confusion and demoralization. I have seen questions asked of myself and of my people. And that is why I will always be vegan: to restore the light to those eyes, to restore the promise of life and to fulfil the one universal value we can build a new planet upon. That value is empathy.

Craig Cline, Salem, Oregon, USA

I will always be vegan because "it's the Golden Rule thing to do". This moral and ethical precept teaches us that we should behave toward others as we would have others behave toward us. Non-vegans conveniently take the word others to mean other humans. Vegans consider others to include ALL members of the animal kingdom, both humans and non-humans alike.

Generally, humans know that the non-human beings we call animals have characteristics, and rights, that are fundamentally similar to those of the human beings we call people. It therefore makes logical sense that the spirit of the Golden Rule should also apply to non-human beings. Non-vegans conveniently permit there to be a disconnect—a barrier—between human rights and animal rights. However, elemental logic suggests that there is no real conflict between these sets of rights. They are not mutually exclusive. In fact, they are mutually inclusive. Humans should be "for" both.

I often use the term "animal wrongs" instead of animal rights. This makes it easier for people to see that they simply do not have the right to perpetrate "wrongs"—either directly or indirectly—against the other sentient beings known as animals. It is morally "right" for humans not only to stand up against wrongs, but also to take personal action to end them. Americans took such action during the civil rights movement in the 1960s; to eradicate the abomination of racism.

Today, we should create a national/international "social justice movement" that focuses on eradicating the abomination of speciesism. It is speciesism that is THE underlying cause of all the exploitive injustice that the human species wreaks upon the non-human species. We're at a point in our human evolution where we must recognize that fact, and DO SOMETHING about it. Consider this compelling quote by Henry Spira: "If you see something that's wrong, you've got to do something about it."

Most vegans understand that the practice of speciesism permits abject cruelty against, and causes the undeserved death of, other sentient beings by human beings. Vegans know that speciesism is wrong. Vegans make a morally and ethically based "crossover". They become "humaneitarians"—humans who live as humanely as they can—in the true spirit of the expanded application of the Golden Rule. Because I so wholeheartedly believe that the vegan lifestyle represents the "Golden Rule way to live", I will always be a vegan.

With peace, non-violence, liberty, and justice for ALL,

Craig Cline

Ardent Animal Advocacy Activist

13

Tim Oseckas, Melbourne, Australia

For 25 years I had been living my life like most other people in my culture and society, consuming the flesh from other animals, their milk, their eggs, their honey, wearing their skin, wearing hair taken from their bodies, using products tested on their bodies, and didn't really reflect on the hurt inflicted on other animals for sport and entertainment, or know about the suffering of animals used to breed "pets". As a teenager I remember my brother bringing the corpses of two rabbits home, with holes in their bodies from the shotgun pellets that had killed them. That night parts of their corpse were served on my plate and I recall feeling very uncomfortable forcing the flesh into my mouth. I knew something wasn't right about this. I had also been taken "fishing" several times as a child, and remember on one occasion seeing a fish thrashing, floundering, gasping on the beach. Another time an older cousin said to me, "Imagine if a giant stepped on you", as I attempted to squash an insect under my foot. I never liked the taste of cow's milk and cheese, so I tried soy milk as an alternative with my breakfast cereal. At one point I convinced myself that eating the flesh of other animals was okay if done "respectfully", like in stories I had been told of the First Peoples who hunted other animals for food.

In 2003 I discovered the Animal Liberation Movement and veganism. I read some articles, watched some videos, and almost overnight I had become a vegan. I cleared out my house of clothing and other products that had been taken from or tested on the bodies of other animals, joined a few organisations, and participated in several protests. I started to tell other people about the realities I had discovered. Several years later my sister, uncle and aunty joined me as a vegan.

Over time, my understanding of the issues has deepened with the aid of further research, discussions, involvement in activism (including open rescues), and learning about speciesism, intersectionality of oppression and other forms of discrimination. I now know that I had been culturally and socially conditioned to accept unnecessary violence as the norm, indoctrinated with a violent ideology, a speciesist belief system that almost all cultures and societies accept without question. I have also come to see the relationship between the exploitation and killing of other animals and human procreation and overpopulation, environmental destruction, capitalism, consumerism, patriarchy, and how many people live in denial of, or choose to ignore, the suffering and killing of other animals because of their religions, culture, traditions, customs, convenience, jobs, beliefs, relationships, and attitudes.

Knowing what I know now, I know I will always be vegan. There is no way I could ever return to living in a way that supports and inflicts unnecessary breeding, abuse, torture, mutilations, and death on other animals.

Susan Cho, Chicago, USA

I will always be vegan:

- Because of the bear trapped in a tiny cage, continuously drained of the bile so prized by humans. The elephant whose family was shot so she could be used in a circus. The lobster who had been guarding her children when she was trapped and boiled alive. And the ground nestlings who were crushed when hay was harvested to feed "happy cows" during winter.

- Because of Fasier; the Siberian tiger, mascot of a university. He lived at an accredited zoo that spearheads international conservation and educational programs. Fasier paced several steps to the end of his cage every day. Then he turned and paced back.

- Because of Anthony, the beloved young goat in a small dairy herd. His legs shook with terror as he was carted off to die. His caretaker cried as the trusting Anthony bleated his bewilderment.

- Because of the mouse who was force-fed laundry detergent until her organs finally failed and she died a miserable death. And the mother and baby macaque wrested away from each other, to study the effects of a human anti-anxiety drug.

- Because of the first male chick of the morning to tumble from the conveyor belt to the grinder below. His sisters will live in a backyard and be called "happy chickens" until they are slaughtered.

- Because of Oscar, Lucas, and Petunia who escaped the grisly fate of millions of pigs. They would have borne their torture in completely different ways, because they are different individuals, with their own personalities.

- Because of the human child who died from dehydration and starvation because the water and land that once sustained her family are now used for cattle, to feed other humans.

- Because of the calf who lived next to a sanctuary and daily tried to push through to freedom and companionship. Every day, the farmer carried him back to the reality of his life (and death) on a "humane farm".

- Because I have been told that the saddest sound in the world is a dairy cow calling to her stolen child.

I have literally billions of compelling reasons to remain vegan all my life. I may falter at times, but exploiting animals deliberately? It's unthinkable.

Melanie Thomet, South Africa

The ONLY thing I am certain of in this life…

They say that the only things that are certain in this life are death and taxes. My imagination begs to disagree. The philosopher in me has debated death—the form of death; the beyond of death; the fear of death—from every angle. There is little about death that seems certain to my mind. Taxes? Sure, I pay mine—but for all I know, I'm simply being duped over and over again with each fiscal year that ushers me closer toward the mystery of death. Nothing about death, nor taxes, seems "certain" to me.

Veganism. Therein lies my only certainty in life. I am CERTAIN that animals are sentient beings who can suffer and have a will to live. They feel; they think; they breathe. I am CERTAIN that harming them in ANY way is a hideous crime—whether or not the State would find me guilty on such charges. I am certain that the furs and skins of my animal brothers and sisters look far more beautiful on them than they ever could on me! I am certain that I could not use cosmetics and detergents that have maimed innumerable innocents through animal testing. I am certain that terms like "circus" and "zoo" are mere euphemisms for animal slavery, disguised by semantics. I am certain that there is no logic that could defend my choice to identify the life of my "pet animal" as priceless, and simultaneously allow me to attach a price tag to the life of a "food animal". The moral code by which I live must be one of consistency. These are the simple consistencies and certainties that veganism adds to my consciousness. I am awakened in veganism. Veganism has ripped the proverbial wool from my eyes. I trust the principles of veganism as it offers the simplest, most comprehensible foundation of morality: In every situation, always do the least amount of harm possible.

I am certain that I want NO hand in the destruction of the Earth, nor to carry guilt upon my shoulders when future generations turn to us and ask us WHY we didn't change our ways when there was still hope. I am certain that I am a minute speck in the cosmos. I do not wear a badge of self-importance that allows me to declare myself hierarchically superior to the other beings alongside whom I wander this globe. In this acknowledgement, I thereby declare that I am by no means entitled to pillage the Earth, or to commodify or enslave the Earth's inhabitants. Instead, my responsibility is to honour, protect and respect all that I am privileged to be a part of in this lifetime.

I am certain that I wish to be known for all that is connected with veganism: compassion and kindness; a clear and consistent ethical code; a sound and solid respect for ALL life forms. I am certain that I do not wish to be known for all that is associated with the alternative: animal suffering; planetary destruction; hypocrisy; ignorance; ethical incongruity; and misplaced notions of human grandeur.

For these reasons, VEGANISM is the ONLY thing I am certain of in this life. For these reasons, I will ALWAYS be vegan!

Butterflies Katz, New Zealand/USA

I've been vegan for 36 years, therefore it is safe to say I will always be vegan. I committed to vegan living before any health benefits of the vegan diet were known. I stopped eating animals at age 12 when I learned "meat" was a dead animal, and became fully vegan immediately upon first reading about the ethic, when I was 21. This demonstrates that I never believed humans have a right to breed, enslave, exploit, and kill animals. I will always find it unethical, and I won't ever want to be complicit in the objectification of feeling beings.

I feel repulsion for all animal-exploiting industries and their disturbing products derived from animal abuse. For example, milk is meant for babies of another species who are killed (just after birth) so people can steal their sustenance. Leather, fur and other fabrics worn by humans come from animals who need their own skin. Somehow it is accepted as normal to eat rotting corpses, or to be entertained by animals stolen from the world they should live in, wrongfully imprisoned, and forced into demeaning (and often harmful) acts, tricks, or labor. I will never want to pay for products that are tested in the eyes of rabbits or to steal the food bees make for themselves. I am not drawn to that way of thinking. I have zero desire to be violent to anyone; human or other animal.

If one is not vegan, they are directly paying for animals to be violently assaulted on their behalf. Long-term vegans are proof we can live vegan; thereby making veganism a social justice issue. I will always want to do my part in advancing humanity to a species that does not intentionally and needlessly violate the inherent rights of conscious, perceptually-aware, feeling beings. Animals that are exploited for human purposes also fear death, desire to nurture their newborn, have families, have eyes and faces, are communicative, and have pain receptors, a brain, and a nervous system which gives them the capacity to suffer.

Through the decades, I've come to see the many far reaching natural outcomes that will result from humans embracing vegan living. Planetary healing and a less oppressive society will replace the environmental degradation caused by farming animals, and the violence that presently plagues our planet. I will always want to be a pioneer of humanity's next step. I strive to live my life guided by the Golden Rule, the principle of nonviolence, and "doing the right thing", therefore I have no choice but to be vegan.

Oscar Horta, Galicia, Spain

Professor of Animal Ethics at University of Santiago de Compostela

Rejecting Speciesist Injustice Towards Non-Human Animals

Veganism means not harming non-human animals for our own benefit. It means, therefore, not acting unjustly towards them. No one would honestly agree to undergo the harms that exploited animals have to go through (mainly, their suffering and their death) in order for us to be able to use the products of their exploitation (that is, to taste their meat, milk, eggs or honey; to wear their skin, feathers, hair or silk; or to enjoy some entertainment by watching them perform, fight, or being locked in jail). Humans use animal products and services only because they are not the ones paying the price for it; non-human animals pay the price. This shows how unjust animal exploitation is, and why it is a form of speciesism; the discrimination against those who don't belong to a certain species.

When it comes to respecting others, what we should take into account is only whether they are sentient and can thus have positive and negative experiences. Neither mere species membership nor complex intellectual capacities are relevant. Note that there are humans who don't have those capacities, such as babies or those with intellectual disabilities, and yet we think they should be fully respected. This should make us realize that the idea that we can discriminate against those who do not have certain cognitive capacities is unacceptable. This is why it is speciesist to harm non-human animals in ways in which we would never accept harming human beings. In fact, giving any kind of arbitrary priority to human interests over those of non-human animals is discriminatory and speciesist.

To be sure, there are other ways in which non-human animals are harmed apart from their use as resources. They commonly suffer and are killed in situations in which humans could help them but refuse to do it, as it often happens in the case of those who die in misery in the wild. This means that rejecting speciesism not only implies ceasing to harm non-human animals, but also entails helping them when they need it, just as we would do it if they were humans.

However, veganism is a very important part of what it means to reject discrimination against non-human animals, as animal exploitation is one of the most important consequences of that discrimination. Fortunately, though, we can all do something about this. We can all oppose injustice. We can reject animal slavery. In other words: we can live vegan.

Clinton Vernieu, Brisbane, Australia

Now that I am awake, I cannot go back to sleep. Awakened from a culturally induced slumber, I have made a pledge to myself—but, more importantly, I have taken an oath for the animals. I am now their caregiver, witness and companion—I will never be able to justify their exploitation. This connection is now embedded deep within my being and there is no going back.

I will stick with being a vegan because it is the tougher road to travel. It would be much easier to stay asleep, and blissfully unaware of what happens behind the walls of the slaughterhouses and testing facilities. Becoming a vegan connected the dots for me, and I can no longer claim ignorance or indifference. Making the connection removes the veil and exposes the reality that society has gone to great lengths to conceal. As a vegan, I view the world through a lens of compassion and empathy. I can now see through the walls and will never again allow myself to be blindfolded or misled by the masses.

For me, veganism is not a fad diet, social club or some kind of life-crisis, attention-seeking hipster ideal. It is a moral philosophy and lifestyle with a foundation of certain principles and tenets. Not all that dissimilar to other "isms" that denote a specific practice, system or philosophy. It is not temporary or just a phase; it will be a lifelong journey of progress and learning. Vegan for life—and for their lives.

Russell Tenofsky, California, USA

Very simply, I refuse to participate as much as possible in the institutionalized exploitation of sentient beings. Their lives matter to them as much as mine does to me. My being vegan makes a very public and political statement that compassion and justice for all beings is imperative if we want to live in a morally evolved society.

19

Theresa Bennett-Hayes, Oregon, USA

My life (and the right to live it) matters to me just as the life of any fellow sentient being matters to them. As humans we are capable of co-existing on this planet peacefully, happily and successfully with all others. There is no reason to be anything other than vegan for life.

Rowena Poitras, Brisbane, Australia

I will always be vegan, so I can stand strong and proud and say that the animals screaming for the torture to stop…are not tortured and murdered in my name.

Photo by Karrel Christopher - www.karrelchristopher.com

Martha Readyoff, USA

There is, for better or worse, a righteousness associated with being vegan. Four years ago when I told people—good friends, even—that I had decided to become vegan, some replied with a shocking bitterness that bordered on resentment. "Well, I guess you're perfect now", I heard more than once. Needless to say I am far, far—far from perfect. It hurt me that people I thought knew me so well would think that of me, that I had placed myself on some self-righteous pedestal and now looked down on them. When I thought past my own hurt, it occurred to me that committing to being vegan is such an obvious force of good and that most people know this even if they're not ready to take it on themselves, so they tend to be defensive. If I had those moments to do again, if I wasn't so caught off guard, I might reply (albeit maybe a little cheekily), "You could be perfect, too! It's fun and easy! Come on, join me."

The truth is, I do feel enlightened. But not in a holier-than-thou sort of way. I know and understand the world in a way that I didn't before, but much of that awareness is heartbreaking. The abject cruelty of factory farming, medical and cosmetic testing, fur farming, etc. has seared in my mind images of defenseless animals punished by unspeakable suffering. Knowledge of far reaching, damaging health and environmental repercussions of these industries of pain, I can't forget. Rather than make me feel better about myself, they serve to remind me how flawed I am, we all are, what dark things we are capable of, and how much work there is to do. Knowing, I cannot forget. Seeing, I cannot close my eyes. Opening my heart to all creatures, I cannot stop it beating. There is righteousness but it comes at a cost, and the only way to repay that debt is to live a life of kindness and compassion.

Fortunately, that part is easy and fun, a joy to do! I have no illusions of becoming Tolstoy, living a life of ascetic privation. I have never lived so abundantly and gratefully as I have since becoming vegan, for now I reverence and celebrate not just my own life but the lives of all animals, solaced by my choice to ease the world's suffering in my small, flawed way.

Dan Cudahy, Colorado, USA

We often presume, without much thought, that we deserve the circumstances of our lives. But let's consider this presumption. We didn't choose to be born. We didn't choose our parents, race, sex, mental capacity, era in history, or our species. All of these are matters of pure luck, and yet largely define our lifelong experience on Earth. Luck is, by far, the largest factor in determining whether we will live human lives in 21st century comfort or luxury; or we'll live lives of unbearable torture and abject misery as a pig, chicken, or other sentient being born into animal agriculture; or somewhere in between, perhaps as a human in poverty.

When we intentionally contemplate the wild arbitrariness and caprice of fortune, it becomes easier to empathize with those less fortunate than ourselves. We realize on a deeper level that, by definition, nobody deserves his or her fortune, regardless of its quality. Cultivating empathy and contemplating our own relative fortune helps break down the strong barrier we unconsciously construct between self and other, and we start to see ourselves as if we were the other, regardless of their race, sex, species, or any other circumstance of birth.

The more we empathize and see ourselves as if we were another sentient being, the more open we are to examining what we can do to help, or at least not contribute to the harm of, other beings—human or non-human—less fortunate than ourselves. We realize that we all have desires. We all want to avoid unnecessary hardship. As sentient beings, we share this condition of wanting contentment. Even those more fortunate than we are worthy of our empathy, for they are more likely to be stuck on the hedonic treadmill: chasing after the next pleasure or preference, only to find boredom or dissatisfaction after a short while, then on to the next chase, and so on.

We also see that taking the well-being of others seriously, while either getting off, or slowing down, our own hedonic treadmill is an incomparably saner and more fulfilling way to live. For me, veganism is an indispensable cornerstone, and a minimum standard, of taking the well-being of others seriously. I could do more, and sometimes do, but being vegan is the very least I can do in taking my ethical commitments seriously. This is why I'll always be vegan.

Mariana Cerovečki, Croatia

Since I was a little child, I have always loved animals—well, I thought I loved "all animals", but in reality I only loved and respected dogs and cats. I ate meat, dairy and other products of animal exploitation. I didn't know better; I didn't make the connection between what was on my plate and the lives that were ended for those meals. But as I grew and found more information, I quickly had a shift in my perspective, my way of life. I slowly started to realize that this was going to be my calling—that I would devote myself to helping animals. I realized it's not enough to volunteer at dog shelters. I wanted to help ALL animals and I realized the first step to do that was to start with myself and my choices—so I made the decision to stop participating in every type of animal exploitation. I became vegan when I was 13 years old, and shortly after that I became an animal rights activist.

Although I was really young, I remember that the only thing I regretted was that I didn't do this earlier. How could I have claimed to love and help animals while I was consuming the products of their suffering? I knew that there was nothing I could do to change the past, so I focused on the future. I knew that being a vegan and animal rights advocate would be my purpose. I devoted every minute of every day to helping animals. I will always be vegan because that is the least I can do for the animals. It is the moral baseline for humanity; it is the only non-violent, egalitarian way of life for both human and non-human persons on this planet.

When I was 13 and had just started as an animal rights activist, I had a vision that the whole world would be vegan if I continued spreading this message. Most people called me "crazy" and "young and naïve". Well, 9 years later, I still have the same vision, but now I don't care if most people think I'm crazy—because it's not about them. I look into the eyes of pigs, chickens, cows and I am reminded why I do it. And in those moments, those moments of friendship and respect between a human and non-human, I'm sure we can achieve this "young and naïve" vision of a vegan world. And if you still think it's crazy, go and spend some time at an animal sanctuary; look into their eyes and try telling THEM a vegan world is not possible.

Julie Hammond, Columbus, Ohio, USA

Be the change you wish to see. The magnitude of wisdom contained within that short sentence is sometimes too overwhelming for people. It can be difficult to stand behind your convictions in a world of complacency and evasiveness. It's easy to go with the flow, not call attention to yourself or your beliefs, not advocate for a seemingly lost cause. Fielding ridiculous questions can sometimes be exhausting, I admit it. In a day and age where you can educate yourself at the click of a button, I tend to wonder why I'm still being asked where I "get my protein from?" Despite the constant questions, raised eyebrows, behind the back snickers, in your face jokes, and anything else that comes with the territory, I will always be vegan. Some might ask why.

The reason is both as simple and as complex as that first sentence. I am being the change that I wish to see. I wish to live in a world where we don't hurt our friends for personal gain. I wish to live in a world where everybody is considered a friend. I wish to live in a world that values a symbiotic relationship. All of these wishes extend beyond the human race. They include every living creature. They even include the limited resources that we are responsible for treasuring and sharing. There is a reason we are all here together. I don't know what that reason is any more than the next person. Deep down, I'd like to think that walking around upright with an air of false superiority and an affinity for greed is not the reason. Maybe I'm wrong. Maybe I'm not. It's what I believe and it's the change I would like to see.

I will always be vegan because I don't find it easier to go with the flow. I find it easier to stand up for what I believe in and make sure that everyone I come in contact with knows how I feel. I will always be vegan because I want to pass that gift on to the next generation. I will always be vegan because I am healthy and strong and I did not have to harm a single living creature to obtain that valuable commodity. There are a multitude of reasons that I will always be vegan. The more pressing question is, when will you start?

Sandra Suárez Ramos, Mexico City, Mexico

Have you ever dreamed of freedom, justice and, overall, a life without violence, discrimination and hatred? This has been a question I have constantly asked myself from a very young age. As a woman born into a male dominant, misogynistic society, I always thought of myself as being a victim of unequal treatment; of a downright discriminative, oppressive culture. Feeling as one of the unfortunate members of the losing side of the game, I armed myself with words and knowledge, doing research on women`s rights, feminism and gender equality, questioning religion, tradition and culture.

However, it was not until I came across animal rights issues that it finally struck me and altered my worldview. My struggle for gender, race and even social equality suddenly changed. I was no longer the victim, nor was I on the side of the oppressed. At that moment I understood and finally accepted that I was the oppressor. Every day, through every single action and choice made, I was inflicting far worse pain on someone else than I had once felt. I was paying others to exploit, abuse, imprison and kill someone else for the sole reason that they were "just" animals. I was a speciesist.

The number of land animals slaughtered for food each year across the world is 3.7 billion; this number does not include marine animals. In addition there are millions who are killed in shelters, used and eventually destroyed in laboratories, victims of fashion who die only so that a human can wear their fur or skin, shot by hunters, or starved to death by irresponsible humans who only see them as an accessory for their home or garden. In total more than 150 billion animals are slaughtered each year worldwide. An appalling number, right?

What does veganism have to do with women's rights and human rights? The answer is as simple as the understanding that no one has any right over anyone else. We do not own other sentient beings, so we have no say in regards to their freedom or their lives; we can only respect their existence and the fact that they are born with an inherent right to life. As long as we cannot understand that, we cannot presume to be evolved beings, and the fight for social justice will remain a dream.

I have chosen veganism for life because I believe in freedom, social justice, and equality. Most important, I respect the life of all sentient beings. I will do whatever I possibly can to help this message spread and get through to all people, so we can finally evolve and live free from harm. We are all earthlings sharing a moment in time and the desire to live and love.

Juliet Gellatley, United Kingdom

In the Dead of Night

I don't find investigating factory farms easy. It does not matter how many times I have clambered over fences in the thick of night drawing towards some ominous concrete ugliness, I always feel a sickness in the pit of my belly. It's not just the thought of confronting what our species does to the animals inside the sheds, it's because I'm frightened for my own safety, and the safety of my friends. I'm not that brave.

It has meant though, that I've looked into the eyes of the animals who are incarcerated. Those who have known nothing but a life of relentless, gnawing pain and utter frustration. What is hard is when they look back. Sometimes they look back like they are trying to work me out, to find an answer in my soul. Hardest to handle is when they plead. I apologise for being human. I feel anger at the abject misery we cause on a global scale, at the despair and sadness at not being able to rescue all the innocent prisoners. But somehow, I hope that by exposing the reality of these hellholes, people will change.

It's tragic that any animals are exploited and abused for food or for any human purpose. The scale of suffering is unimaginable. One example of how we treat pigs personifies the callousness of factory farming. Birth is magical. But not when it takes place in a cage only inches bigger than the mother's body; so small she can barely move and can never turn around. What should be beautiful and rewarding becomes horribly obscene. To me, the thought of such cruelty and deprivation is unbearable—particularly when repeated over and over again, year after year. Of course, whether factory farmed or not, it is cruel that she was turned into a baby machine. This mother and her babies, objectified into "things" to be at our disposal. It is horrendous that we treat our fellow earthlings in this way.

Abusing animals is wrong. If we have no empathy with them and respect for the natural world, what are we? I feel to my core that if we demean any part of nature, because we are part of nature, it means demeaning ourselves. Veganism is central to saving all animals, both farmed and wild. In fact, the number one cause of loss of species worldwide is the consumption of meat, fish and dairy.

Veganism is one of the few individual acts we can all perform that has an immediate impact. It is one of the biggest steps any of us can take to heal the planet. To end cruelty. It is also a political act and a clear expression of a belief in a different way of doing things, and a different kind of world—a better world. Yes, I'll always be vegan!

Salwa Maddad, Al-Sweida, As-Suwayda, Syria

In 2010, a new awareness arose within me and guided me to be vegan. I am fully aware that a person's actions and behavior can change the people around them. My daughters and 25 of my friends became vegan at that time. Now there are more than 100 persons that are vegan, just in my region. My granddaughter is also raised vegan by a vegan father and mother.

Most people think the vegan way is complex and difficult, but for me it was so easy. I found the alternatives in a short time. Vegan food is delicious and various. I prepare all recipes at home because vegan products are not available in my country.

Some people think veganism is a diet, but actually it is a way of living; it is the morally right thing to do. We can't live happy and healthy while harming other beings. Although the animals are being killed and are suffering, we should not share in this negative circle. We are sharing in this by our ignorance. When we experience this internal awakening, we will know the reality that every being has the same essence, but each soul wears a different form. When we reach the threshold of mercy and compassion, we cannot support any process involving damage to, and suffering of, any sentient being.

The humane should understand the fact that the animals are not born to be food or products for them. We should not interfere in the ending of animals' lives, nor use animals as our things, for entertainment, or any other purpose. We should not support industries based on animals.

There are many videos about how animals are suffering. They show them trying to run away; cues that they want to protect their life. All of them resist death. The ugliest sight is of people taking calves from cows immediately after they were born, so they can't drink milk from their mothers. The cows suffer and are later killed for their flesh. The cow's milk is designed for calves, not humans. Dairy products are harmful to our health. The vibration of suffering and killing is transferred to our consciousness which affects our behavior and actions.

Living vegan contributes to a better world and to world peace. Veganism helps us to elevate our values of kindness, compassion, purity, wisdom, and respect, so that our love includes all beings on Earth.

27

Uday Bhobe, Mumbai, India

It was New Year's Day, 2013, a month after my 53rd birthday. On a whim, I made a resolution to go vegan (or so I thought, I now know it was merely a resolution to try a plant-based diet). (I make New Year's resolutions every year. They usually last a couple of weeks.) An omnivore since birth, I had encountered several excellent articles and speeches by eminent doctors and dieticians. The health benefits of a plant-based diet were obvious to me.

My new diet was working very well. I live in Mumbai, but was in the US on a longish business trip (5 months). I started reading more about veganism. The ethical side of veganism made compelling sense to me. The logic was clear and irrefutable. Non-human animals are on this planet WITH us and not FOR us. We do not have the moral right to use them for any purpose—never mind murder them, rape them, or steal their milk, eggs and babies. We have no right to treat them as our property.

It was probably around January 20, less than 3 weeks after my New Year's resolution, that I had a flash of insight—a moment of awakening. It was like one of those optical illusions, where you look at a picture of a very old woman, and suddenly see the young girl too. In that instant, I understood what veganism really was. In that instant I knew I would always be vegan.

I remember feeling depressed for a while. How could I have missed this simple truth? How could I have chosen to consume animal products for 53 years? Oh well, better late than never, I consoled myself. Soon I extended my veganism to clothing and household goods. I also began to tell my friends and family about veganism.

I educated myself about the differences between animal welfare (typified by single issue campaigns) and animal rights (characterized by the abolitionist approach and an uncompromising stance towards veganism as a moral baseline). I read articles and watched documentaries about speciesism. It became clear to me that veganism was the only antidote to speciesism. I now believe that veganism is the minimum standard of decency, and do my bit to spread veganism.

This is one New Year's resolution that I will never break in my life.

Vegan for life—for the animals.

Petra Sindelarova, **Prague, Czech Republic**

I grew up as a "normal" child. I used to like animals just like the people around me. Animals were cute and fun to play with. During the summer holidays, which I would spend at a cottage with my grandparents, we would have rabbits, chickens, or geese. I remember getting very close to them; playing all day long with my best friends. When the day came for them to be killed, I was crying, angry, but then accepted it, and forgot about it with time. I ate what was given to me and did not think much about it.

When I was 13 years old, I accidentally saw a TV programme about factory farming and slaughtering animals for food. I was horrified. I just could not believe what I saw. All that screaming, blood, fear, violence and the whole machinery of treating animals as if they were products. It broke my heart. I could not understand how we humans could be so cruel. Why had no one ever told me about it? Was it a taboo? I cried the whole night and said to my parents I could not eat meat anymore.

I started to research more about factory farming and the use of animals in general. There was not that much literature available back then. I was the only vegetarian I knew. Then I decided I had to improve the welfare of animals, so that at least they could experience less suffering when being used by humans. I went to study at the University of Agriculture in the hope that I could learn more about how to help animals. What a naivety. Instead they were teaching us how to make good profits by using animals.

When I was 27, I did an internship at a farm sanctuary in California which shifted me to another level: from being brainwashed about the necessity of using animals to a clear realisation that animals are not ours to use at all. The direct contact with rescued animals made me go vegan without a second thought.

My understanding of our exploitation of animals continued to grow. In 2012 my friend and I started a Czech branch of an international movement that aims for freedom for all animals. Now we have thousands of supporters and many great activists who help us do demonstrations and inform the general public about the reality.

We are also opening The Farm of Hope; the first farmed animal sanctuary in the Czech Republic. I believe there is a hope. I look back and see where I started; watching one short documentary on TV as a small girl, not knowing anyone who would understand. And now I see thousands of devoted activists, hundreds of vegan restaurants and ethical businesses. People are opening their minds. There is a big change going on. And I believe one day I will be telling my grandchildren stories about times when humans used to exploit and eat animals. And they will listen with eyes wide open in amazement.

Ven. Tashi Nyima, Puerto Rico

Dark Alleys, Bright Aisles

Having abandoned the taking of life, refraining from the taking of life, we dwell without violence, with the knife laid down, scrupulous, full of mercy, trembling with compassion for all sentient beings.

Buddha Shakyamuni

When people think of Buddhist monks, they imagine that we dwell in clouds of incense, smiling serenely, unperturbed, meditating on nothing. However, we are not called to drift placidly in emptiness, but to "tremble with compassion for all sentient beings".

Late one night some years ago, my Teacher and I passed by a dark alley and heard the cries of fear and pain of a youth who was being beaten by a gang. Without hesitation, my Teacher approached the men and, smiling broadly, asked them if it would not be much more "fun" to beat up two Buddhist monks instead of one young man.

I was not smiling broadly. I was not smiling at all. You see, Buddhist monks vow not to resort to violence, even to defend ourselves. We do not fight. We were going to get pummelled. Surprisingly, the beating stopped, the men laughed nervously, uttered some choice profanities, and left.

I asked my Teacher if he had known that we would not come to harm. He responded that he did not, but at the very least, we could have taken some of the blows, and not all would have fallen on that one young man. And then he told me soberly that it was our sacred duty, whenever confronted with suffering, to get in the way, to stand between those who would do harm and those who would be hurt.

Not all abuse happens in dark alleys. Much unspeakable cruelty takes place in the brightly lit aisles where we purchase the flesh of animals, their eggs, their milk, their skin, their wool, their feathers, and their fur. Those brightly lit aisles conceal the horrible darkness where animals are confined, enslaved, tortured, and slaughtered for our pleasure.

I implore you to look upon ALL our fellow sentient beings, human and non-human, with compassion. If we cannot prevent the cruelty they suffer, at least let harm not be inflicted for our pleasure, paid for with our money, and executed in our name. Compassion begins in our shopping carts, in our closets, in our kitchens, and on our plates—now and always!

Amanda Benham, Brisbane, Australia

L is for Lamb so soft and sweet,
the alphabet book made no mention of meat.
But "Eat your lamb, it's so delicious",
made my young mind quite suspicious.

Surely it's not really a dear young creature,
that our Sunday meal has as the feature?
"But you must eat your meat or you will die",
my mother repeated the well-worn lie.

So like many others I became complicit,
in a system where violence is implicit.
And when I later saw how animals are abused,
my heart was heavy and my mind confused.

As in my vet studies they'd clearly said,
"Without meat and dairy we'd all be dead."
So often was this lie repeated,
the truth was hidden, and I felt defeated.

But then I chanced upon a woman, clearly alive,
who said "Without animal products we can thrive."
She looked not sickly, but healthy and strong,
and I already knew animal use was wrong.

*Photo by El Hogar ProVegan
animal sanctuary, Spain -*
www.elhogarprovegan.org

From that day on to my beliefs I became true,
the products of animal use I'll always eschew.
Like us, animals want to live their own lives,
and not end up on our forks and knives.

So for many years I studied human nutrition,
as part of my plan for total abolition.
I wanted to kill that convenient lie,
that on animal products humans must rely.

To take away every single excuse,
that people make for animal use.
I vowed to be both clear and strong,
in helping to right a terrible wrong.

I'm vegan for life because it is in my soul,
and liberation for all—my ultimate goal.

Brook Katz, South Florida, USA

As a man of logic and reasoning, it was a natural choice for me to go into the sciences. I moved towards the fields of medicine. It seemed natural to watch someone be fillet open and having body parts removed, and then go to lunch and have a big burger or slab of animal muscle laid in front of me to eat. The science had taught me that we were meat eaters and that was the most efficient way to get the 100 grams of protein a day that we needed. It also taught me that the greatest source of calcium and other nutrients was the lactose bovine solution from the udders of cows, and that if I didn't have at least 25% of my daily intake from this source I would become somehow deficient and possibly put my life at risk. These were facts! So we were told. Back then I didn't connect the dots to see how much money influenced all these so called "facts". I believed in the science and science couldn't be wrong, it was science! As I reached the almost 300lb mark on my scale, and suffering from an array of maladies, I had an epiphany. The logical side of me said the science isn't working right.

My sister, a long time ethical vegan, had touted for years about the moral and ethical side of veganism, but I brushed her off because she didn't have the science to back up anything she said. I called it the "fluff", when people play to your emotional side rather than the reasoning side. But a change did need to happen and I didn't know what, or even where to turn.

Then I met my mentor, my friend, and the person who opened my eyes to the truth, Dr. Michael Klaper. He pulled me through the looking glass and I've never turned back. He showed me the science was biased because of the economics. We studied the true anatomy and physiology of the human body and realized all the numbers were skewed because of the animal industries. Years of scientific research have now shown us that humans need way less protein, get way too much fat, and have absolutely no need at all for that substance called "dairy". We have learned that most of the harm done to the body is from what we put in it. The strange thing was that I found myself in an almost Darwinian evolution. I found that as I no longer had to kill an animal for food, the need for the rest of the body parts also seemed less logical. To just use an animal for its skin or glandular fluids seemed wasteful.

Then it happened. It was such a natural progression that I didn't even realize it. I found myself in touch with not only the animals, but the environment, and water conservation, global warming, health issues, and worst of all, feelings! I started feeling for anyone and everything. It was like something had moved me to a different level of awareness. Like I had climbed the next rung on the evolutionary ladder.

So why will I stay vegan the rest of my life? Because I continue to move up that ladder and going backwards is not my direction or a possibility. As I approach my 30th year of veganism, logic still dictates my mind, but compassion now rules my heart. Thank you to all who helped make it happen.

Bianca Zvorc Morris, Slovenia

Founder, *BeeZeeEcoLand.com* (ethical, vegan business)

My journey into my love and fight for animals started even before I was born, in a small town called Murska Sobota, Slovenia. For some reason, when my mom became pregnant with me, eating meat made her sick. Despite doctors being upset with her, she ignored them. When I was old enough to eat foods beside her breast milk, she tried giving me liver (the pediatrician was telling her that I would become anemic). I kept spitting the meat out and she gave up on me. At age one, I became vegetarian by my own wish. I refused to eat meat in school even though it meant being yelled at by kitchen staff and teachers, and constantly teased by other students. Life was hard, but I could not stand the smell of meat; foul, rotten, and dead.

When I was eight, I found a dog in a garbage can. He was the most perfect being on this planet, and he became my best friend who loved me unconditionally. At age 14, I started working at a local animal shelter and became obsessed with saving animals. At age 16, somebody gave me a book that helped me decide to stop being part of the massive murder of innocent helpless beings: animals, my best friends. I became vegan.

I fell into temptation when I met my husband who was a meat and egg eater just to be "big" and athletic. I tried cheese and butter, but threw up a few hours later. Instead of trying to be more like him (and others), I told him the truth about animal slavery and begged him not to be a part of it. I sent him videos and articles. It was a year of transitioning, but he is now a super athletic and passionate vegan.

Humans are animals that need to learn how to live in tune with nature and other earthlings. We occupy this planet, destroying and killing; including our own planet. Consuming and abusing other earthlings is wrong and makes absolutely no sense; it is insane. My biggest wish in life is to see a vegan world before I die. The breeding of animals would be illegal globally. Animals would have freedom and the right to live and love their families. Then I could be truly proud of being a part of the human species. I will be vegan for the rest of my life because it is the only right thing to do.

Carol Williams, **United Kingdom**

I was raised to eat animals, just like most children in our society. I spent 58 years condemning sentient beings to lives of ruthless exploitation that would end in brutal death. For a few years I was vegetarian and then lapsed back into my old habits. I have no excuses for any of this and will make none. I am guilty. I paid people to kill animals so that I could eat them, just as my parents taught me to do. Like most people I did not question it. Now I am vegan, I have to make up for lost time, make amends, try to educate other people. There is not a second to lose. This is the most important moral revolution in the whole of our history.

I have been involved in the environmental movement for many years but not once have any of the organisations which I support encouraged veganism. Friends of the Earth will campaign tirelessly for greener energy, more recycling and fewer roads but never once mention the contribution animal farming makes to climate change and resource depletion; never once profile its unsustainability.

Similarly—world hunger. Not once have I been advised, by any of the Third World Aid charities I support, to go vegan and free up more food for people. This, despite the fact that 40,000 children die every day for lack of food while the privileged eat animals who have been fed the grain that could have fed these children. It is a scandal that few seem willing to confront.

I have always wept over the suffering of neglected horses and abused dogs, despised "country sports" and been horrified by vivisection, fur farming, whale slaughter and so forth. I see now, at last, that there is no difference between all of this and farming animals. All of it is horribly wrong.

I will always be vegan because now, at last, I understand that other animals are not, and never have been, a "resource" for human use. We have committed a crime against them. It is time to evolve away from this way of being. The future has to be vegan, or there can be no future. This is nothing more—or less—than Truth.

Anastasia Zeller, Kazakhstan

When thinking of Kazakhstan, most people probably associate it with wide steppe landscapes, horse-riding nomads and yurts in a remote countryside. This is what it used to be hundreds of years ago. The roaming nomad lifestyle did not allow people to grow plants but to breed cattle, which is not bound to a specific location. Therefore their diet was mainly based on meat and dairy products. Over time, nomad tribes, as well as many other ethnic groups, settled in Kazakhstan and built a culturally diverse society. By the time I grew up, the majority of rural households had their own vegetable garden and animal farm; mostly on a small scale. So did my family. Our diet included plenty of fruit and vegetables, while animal products (especially meat) were only served on special occasions.

Things changed in 1996 when my family immigrated to Germany, where animal products are available everywhere and are affordable for everyone. Suddenly, meat became part of our daily menu. For a long time I did not question our eating habits. As the issue of animal abuse and the ecological effects of mass animal farming gained more public attention, I started to rethink the relationship between human and non-human animals. At that point it was not possible for me to ignore the connection between the meat on my plate and the suffering animal anymore.

Even I had doubts about whether I would be able to change my habits. I soon realized that veganism is enrichment rather than sacrifice. My decision to go vegan was like planting a seed of critical thinking and self-reflection. In terms of my diet, it opened my eyes to new and diverse recipes and foods. However, the decision not only affected the food on my plate. From soap to shoes to medicine to furniture, I stopped consuming any kind of products with animal testing and/or animal-based ingredients. It helped me to live more consciously and to take responsibility for my actions. Instead of following the path of consumerism I am now living a more simple life, in which less is more and happiness is gained from giving rather than taking.

Veganism is not only enhancing empathy for all living beings, it is also encouraging us to take responsibility for our environment. In my eyes, this is essential to make a future life for all beings possible.

In the morally progressive state of mind I am in today, not being vegan is unimaginable.

Akiko Iwasa, Japan

I can say with conviction and without any hesitation that I will always be a vegan. I still remember very clearly when I became free from the brainwashing we are all subjected to about the necessity of eating animals. I was truly shocked, angry, and in despair. How could we all be living such a lie?

Until that moment, I didn't think I had any choice about eating animals. In Japan, we are taught in primary school that animal products are absolutely indispensable to human health. We are told we cannot be healthy, build our muscles, or have healthy blood and bones without eating animals. Until then, I was like most people and just followed and obeyed what I was told.

In my heart though, I had always loved animals. I actually chose to study veterinary science at university. There was no internet when I was growing up. In Japan, we rarely get exposed to different ideas or any information other than what is the cultural norm. In school, at work, and even among friends there is tremendous pressure to conform and be the same as everyone else. Without questioning much, I trusted my teachers and textbooks, which offered very limited information about nutrition.

Fifteen years ago, I finally woke up and discovered the facts about how animals are tortured and abused, and all of the negative effects for us and the environment as well.

After I became a vegan, my own health improved a great deal. A uterine fibroid tumor I had for years quickly vanished. My skin problems disappeared. My skin became smooth and healthy. My terrible menstruation pains were gone and I received many other benefits from my vegan diet. I even got pregnant and had a beautiful baby boy.

But the most important thing for me is that I no longer was a part of the violence and exploitation of innocent animals. Since 2003, I have been running one of the largest annual plant-based festivals in Kyoto, Japan. When we started, most people had never heard the word "vegan" in Japan. I'm very happy to say that the situation is changing and veganism is gaining recognition day by day. I have made a lot of wonderful friends with whom I share a common vision of a vegan animal-friendly world. I will continue to introduce people to the virtues of a vegan life here in Japan and around the world.

Diego Andrade Yáñez, Santiago, Chile

In every society that has developed philosophy, there seems to have been people who cared about animals, e.g. in China, Ancient Greece, India, and so on. But it wasn't until Jeremy Bentham that we found a compelling argument against animal abuse; and only with the advent of neuroscience that we gathered evidence to support that idea empirically.

Bentham's argument was simple: it is not our ability to reason or speak which gives us our status as moral patients, but our capacity to suffer. It was said in passing and, to the best of my knowledge, he was not vegetarian, but this was the seed that would later become a respectable area of philosophical inquiry.

The sciences of the mind and brain showed us beyond reasonable doubt that many other animals (especially, mammals and birds) have minds similar to our own. Now we know many other animals have similar neural pathways, neurotransmitters and hormones to those that modulate pain in humans. In suffering, we are the same.

However, all this knowledge would be useless in the absence of technology and a market for it. The willingness and ability to innovate, and the technologies to make it possible, have brought what was once an endeavor restricted to a few philosophically-inclined minds with a lot of willpower to the lives of practical men and women. Veganism is everywhere now and it most likely won't stop spreading. Meatless substitutes are flooding the markets and more people than ever are opting for cruelty-free lifestyles. Science and technology have created fortified foods and supplements, and have allowed the production of insulin without animals.

Someday, not long into the future, in-vitro meat and other animal products (such as cheese or milk or leather) will be sold. These will be truly "cruelty-free": tissues that will have never been a part of an animal in any way, i.e. tissues grown in a laboratory. This will radically change the practice of veganism, but not its essence. As long as animals are not enslaved in the process, it won't matter. Sentient animals' well-being and the freedom to live their own lives is what matters. And so, I will remain a vegan because the whole world will join us and be vegan too.

Cathy Duffield, Whangarei, New Zealand

I am vegan because I do not believe humans can justify, on any grounds, the eating or using of animals. We are one part of an ecosystem in which all life is connected, and therefore the daily choices we make in terms of how we live affects more than ourselves. The idea that we are all connected is based on the concept of the oneness of life. All religions, and many cultures, make reference, at least historically, to this oneness. As we are all "one", to hurt someone is to hurt everyone, including oneself. Pollution from animal industries is an example of this—it adversely affects us all, and not just those who participate, either as producers or consumers (or both), in these businesses.

With the advent of "civilisation" humans began viewing themselves as separate from both other living beings and the Earth itself. Yet we are no more separate from each other than a wave is from the ocean. This belief that we are separate has led to many people acting in ways they perceive to be in their best interests and with little regard for others. We see this in man's treatment of animals. Each year seventy billion animals, bred to produce a range of "products" for human consumption, lead short and tortured lives. Animal industries also create food shortages for many of the world's people, and impact negatively on human health and the environment. Were we all to view ourselves as citizens of the Earth, or earthlings, and our lives as connected, we would not knowingly harm any other living being. We would be vegan.

For me, to not be vegan would mean living without a conscience, and life would become meaningless and without joy. As George Bernard Shaw said, "This is the true joy in life, the being used for a purpose recognised by yourself as a mighty one" and "I am of the opinion that my life belongs to the whole community, and as long as I live it is my privilege to do for it whatever I can." Vegans view animals not as inferior beings with whom we can do as we please, but as individuals very like us, whose lives matter, and who should have the right to live free of exploitation. Animal rights has become a strong unstoppable social justice movement. I wish to continue playing a part in this force for positive change and therefore will always be vegan.

Amanda Beatty, England

I once believed I was an animal lover, yet I had no idea what love really was. I never saw the cruelty I inflicted by what I ate, used or wore; causing so much suffering without a thought. I followed blindly what I had been told, by parents, teachers, governments and media. Then one day I woke up. I couldn't bear to be part of the problem anymore. I saw who we really are and the pain we cause. I will never go back to who I was, because this is who I am and will be forever more.

Where you see meat and eggs, I see others butchered and ground up alive. Animals suffocated, babies dragged from their mothers, or imprisoned and without hope. Your glass of milk or slice of cheese screams rape, abuse, and abduction to me. How can I take a bite of that when every mouthful screams of suffering in my head? When you wear the skin of another, I see animals screaming in pain while their skin hangs off. Why would I wear their skin when I have my own? Trillions of insects are used for a multitude of purposes when none are needed by the human race. When you ride another animal, I ask, "How would you feel if someone treated you like that?" There is no difference between any of us, as we are all animals. When you want a feathery down quilt, I see geese standing in pain and blood. You want to look pretty and unreal; all I see are others needlessly tested on for the sake of vanity. We are killing all others, ourselves, and our planet.

So why would I choose this when there are so many other options that do not cause suffering and death? Why would I put others through that unnecessarily? Yet, in my mind, I would rather see all this than know I am part of the cause. Once you know, really know, there is no going back. So keep in mind that no matter what you say, I have the facts on my side. I am on the side of truth and justice, and for this reason I will always be a vegan.

Photo by El Hogar ProVegan animal sanctuary, Spain - www.elhogarprovegan.org

Daniel Bothma, Johannesburg, South Africa

Although I detest the baggage being "vegan" comes with, I AM NOW AWAKE and wear the label proudly, albeit with that little word "abolitionist" added to the front. I no longer see a difference between piglets and puppies, and the only movie that made this brave son of Africa cry was *Earthlings*. I've always felt an intense reverence toward animals, but that's only part of the reason why I choose to be "maladjusted" to this profoundly sick society. "Veganism" is not a diet, a flash-in-the-pan trend, or some freaky new age cult. Going vegan is a journey few ever have the compassion, discipline and conviction to embark upon. However, I did my homework and discovered that the cheese, milk, eggs, bacon, and steak I was stuffing my face with were all slowly killing me.

Despite the shimmering neon screens proclaiming the opposite, we live in the digital dark ages where might is right and silence is paid for in blood. Everything we think we know about protein, pills, GMOs, and "free-range, happy meat" is propaganda, and loving animals does not mean you have to hate humans. What still baffles me is how people don't realize that you cannot "fight" for compassion. Cruelty and violence in any form begets more horror-shock cruelty and ultra-violence. I did not choose to stop hunting, devouring, and exploiting my fellow creatures because some "Big Green Brother" with black budgets kept trying to guilt, shame, shock, and coerce me into feeling something.

Ultimately, my choice comes down to two simple ideas: I want to live and let live, and I refuse to partake of genocide. If that means lentil soup, tempeh burgers, and home-made mushroom Biltong (Jerky), instead of SOMEONE's tortured and slaughtered babies on my plate, so must it be. A wise old Sangoma once told his young apprentice an ancient tale about the battle we face. Inside every human heart there rages two lions. The dark lion feeds on misery, fear, and death while the lighter lion lives on compassion, light, and love. The boy asked the shaman which lion will win. He replied, "The lion you feed."

My body is clean, my conscience is clear, and my will unbreakable. How about yours?

Alexey Shulga, Moscow, Russia

Although there are many differences between animals and humans we have an important shared ability—the ability to experience pain and distress. Every living sentient being—human or non-human—strives to avoid suffering, any harm, pain or oppression, and wants to live and does not want to die. Every living sentient being values her life even when no one else does. This is the fundamental ethical basis for the moral equality of humans and non-humans. Thus animals matter morally. Therefore, we cannot justify eating, wearing, or using them as resources and a means to human ends. Moreover, we must completely abolish animal exploitation, legally recognize them as persons, and accord them fundamental rights, including the right to live and the right not to be treated as property.

Animals have all sorts of needs and desires as humans do—to live a good life, to communicate with their own kind, to play, to create families and have babies. Thus if my beloved animal brothers and sisters have the same fundamental needs as I do, then it is a matter of fundamental justice—not just compassion—to recognize they are not things and to stop using them as slaves.

My heart and my conscience got restless when I became aware of the horrible truth of animal exploitation. There is always an inner nagging pain knowing that my beloved vulnerable animal friends are enslaved and subjected to slaughter.

We owe them veganism. Veganism is the only rational and moral response to the injustice and horror of animal exploitation. You are either a vegan or you directly participate in imposing suffering and death on animals.

What else should I devote my life to knowing that there is slavery of living beings? Only to a life-long commitment to spread the word of veganism and the abolition of animal exploitation. For nothing else makes any sense until there is no more suffering and oppression of innocent animals on planet Earth.

A human's true ethics is a borderless responsibility for every being that lives. It is the consciousness of the unity of all the living cosmos. I dream of the day when there is no slavery of living beings and no animal suffers. I dream of the day when we stop bringing them into existence in order to betray and slaughter them. I dream of the day when the whole of mankind will turn abolitionist vegan. And I am committed to bringing us nearer to such times.

41

Peter Smith, Vancouver, Canada

Ladies and gentlemen of the jury, we need no introduction to the accused; they are sentient dwellers of this world (like you or I). They are unique, varying in shape and size; in the manner which they move; or how they interact with this planet. We dub them: "animals".

Humankind acknowledges our coexistence on this Earth, our home, with these beings, who neighbour us across this great expanse. And as humans, we acknowledge our distinction, our uniqueness from these creatures. Yet, through some misguided notion, we as a species believe we are entitled to this Earth more than the other earthlings; and, these creatures and their experiences in life must be guided by our hand. We determine their fate... and the question of our own humanity.

In our species' existence, we have thrived from these creatures, exploiting them for their sustenance and warmth in clothing. Justifications of survival were the norm for a long time. In this modern day and age, amongst civilizations interconnected, we are beyond the days of survivalism, and can flourish without cruelty for our foods and our garments. Despite the call for empathy and freedom for animals, nutrition through kinder plant-based sources, and release from our exploitative holds, the atavistic notion of superiority still reigns—the belief that we are the ones to shepherd these animals.

Under this premise, we may touch their existence with compassion or cruelty. We have a choice; they never had one. If humankind has assumed the role of guardian of this planet and all who call it home, then are we not to enrich their lives, or leave them be, instead of consuming them for all their worth? We deduce their value from how we may use them: to be confined in captivity for our entertainment; bred for slaughter and food; killed for sport and fashion; and to be specimens in our experiments. We spread suffering instead of compassion, and needlessly harm and condemn these animals and our home with these horrible practices.

Once upon a time, I stood trial to my conscience and pleaded guilty for my participation in this immoral system. Knowledge of these horrors cannot be unlearned, and cruelty, to creatures who experience the world feelingly like you or I, cannot be supported. My pathway is a vegan life, which I wholeheartedly embrace.

Alannah Quinn, Brisbane, Australia

There was a time when I was unconscious, wrapped up in superficial wants. My mind was fixed on my materialistic needs. I existed purely in a little bubble of simple self, warm in the comfort of my easy ignorance and unable to see the horrific truths of the world through the walls of my self-inflicted coma. I never knew I was ignorant. In fact I prided myself on being intelligent and knowledgeable, believing I was well rounded and in tune with society because I watched the news. I thought I was an environmental activist because I cared about the planet and attended street rallies. I thought I was an advocate for animals because I disapproved of abuse and neglect. I thought I was a humanitarian because I took part in the 40 Hour Famine. I thought I knew all there was to know about life.

Something I have always known, however, is that I want to "save the world". It wasn't until I awoke from this coma that I realized what saving the world actually meant. Some vegans describe their moment of awakening as a "spiritual" experience; others as a "light bulb moment". For me it was like getting whacked in the face with a shovel, having my heart and soul ripped out, and my mind detonated into a million little pieces. It was like being pushed off the edge of a cliff into a black hole I thought may be there, but never truly acknowledged. It was violent, frightening and traumatic, and it was heart breaking. Suddenly you are aware of the animal holocaust happening right now and the mass destruction humans are inflicting on the Earth. Suddenly you become fully aware of the impact your decisions are having on innocent beings and you can't look the other way. There is no choice but to change. You are filled with a passion friends and family don't share, fully understand or appreciate. You are labeled "radical", "difficult to feed", "eco-terrorist", "crazy" and "weird". But the pain knowledge brings you, the labels they pin on you, and the misconceptions they have don't worry you because you are vegan. You are fully aware of what is happening in the world and you have the courage, insight and the heart to acknowledge the facts and to actually do something with them.

Becoming vegan means adopting a philosophical lifestyle that extends beyond the dinner plate. Being vegan means accepting the transformation as an obligation rather than a choice. When you have your "awakening moment", you become aware of the duty you have to create change. This transformation has allowed me to see that wilful ignorance is death to the soul and that living in truth is the only way to exist. I can never return to seeing the world through childlike, ignorant eyes. That's why I'll be a vegan until the day I die.

Ramilyn P. Delposo, Philippines

Filipina living in India

There was a time when a girl, with her family, grew chickens. She trapped one or two to sell for money or dinner. She wove coconut leaves and made them into chicken nests. Some of the eggs were for breakfast—boiled or scrambled. The rest were kept for meat and money.

There was another time when she went to the woods to find wild taro leaves—as foods for pigs. Yes, she fed pigs. Plenty of times! She cleaned their pens, too. She also watched each one of them grow big, be weighed, and get sold. They screamed loudly, especially when their legs were tied. She feasted on them, too, on every special occasion, in varied dishes, served with pride and joy!

Then this same girl carried kittens from their house to a forest and left them there. Whether they were old enough to survive on their own or not, she didn't bother to know! The people around her just wanted those kittens, whose mother kept stealing fish from their pantry, out of their sight!

Three decades have passed and something has changed!

This woman, whose young heart was deadened and made to function by cultural machines, woke up from a deep coma. Her heart started to beat perfectly, the way it should have been. Instead of being welcomed, many have become upset and angry with her.

Why? Because she was reborn!

Those eggs and chickens are no longer valued as money or food. They are now her friends free to experience life.

For her, those pens are now prison cells built like a highly secured facility with a purpose of making the guilty of murder suffer the same fate as the murdered innocents. That scream she heard, which is now clear to her, was actually a cry, a cry for help; a plea for anyone to hear, which then not one ever did.

That momma cat is no longer a cat that steals. She is now a cat that is just claiming her fair share, for she and her kittens have been deprived of what was rightfully theirs for so long. Cats are now her family, the best friends she never had.

Not many really like what she has become! But who is she?

It is I! And I'll always be vegan for I am reborn and able to see the truth—truth that set me free from believing there is pride and joy in oppressing other beings.

Rachel Lena, Peeblesshire, Scotland

Without pretension or any sense of being disingenuous, I am a vegan. This is not something I will change because it is not a choice; it is something I am compelled to do by my nature. Who I am morally rejects living in a different way, and as such I found it natural to become vegan. Changing would feel extreme and would stop me from feeling at home in my own skin. If sometimes feeling out of place in society is the price for feeling at peace with myself, then I am more than willing to compromise.

In regards to the criticism from others who think this life choice will not make a difference, I quote Helen Keller: "I am only one, but still I am one. I cannot do everything, but still I can do something; and because I cannot do everything, I will not refuse to do something that I can do." This is the way that I will live; in hope that others will also see that they can make change. That living contrary to your belief is in itself a contradiction to living.

People can numb to what is ordinary or common, it is the nature of our species. I hope that when someone who has numbed, and perhaps never considered the question on their moral conscience, will begin to contemplate it upon meeting me or others who live life in the same way. I will not numb to witnessing anyone in a state of suffering or death. And so, for as long as I have life, I will live it by my nature as a vegan.

Photo by C-A-L-F Sanctuary, United Kingdom

Ruth Sanderson-Dredge, England

To most people, the idea of knowing that you will always do something is childish and immature; but with veganism it is quite the opposite. One day you realise that using non-human animals in any way is morally wrong. One day a light bulb comes on in your head and you know it never will go off.

A lot of people call themselves "vegan" but never actually make the connection; they never realize exactly what veganism means. To be vegan means non-humans are not ours to cause unnecessary suffering to, ever! It doesn't mean that you eat plant-based but occasionally consume fish. It doesn't mean you are plant-based but, you know, if your friend *really* wants you to go to an animal park, you do. To be vegan means that using non-humans isn't up for discussion. It is as morally problematic as child abuse is for non-vegans (and vegans).

The day the light went on in my head was the best and most scary day of my life. I knew I would never be the same, and I would always strive towards a world where being vegan is the norm not an exception; where those who use animals would be seen as extreme. A world where people would see that it is the non-vegans who push their views on others: the animals (both human and non-human) they exploit.

Drawing by Jo Frederiks - www.jofrederiks.com

Patti Nyman, Toronto, Canada

We live on a beautiful, abundant planet, gifted with bodies that are able to survive and thrive without the death of other sentient beings. Veganism is my way of honouring the gift of life and returning this gift by honouring all other life. Once I was able to fully embrace that animals are beings and not things, that they have their own interests and purposes, I could not un-know this truth. Like learning that Santa Claus is not real, it's like I always knew, and there's no going back. Being vegan has allowed my mind to grow and flourish, no longer encumbered by blocked connections, blocked intuition, blocked compassion, and the series of rationalizations and excuses needed to maintain these blocks. I've developed an increasing openness and appreciation for life, a gratitude that I was not able to fully embrace when I was still within the mindset of taking and reluctantly harming. I rejoice in grasping the beauty and uniqueness of other beings and becoming more completely who I already am.

To others, veganism can appear as restriction. But for me and other committed vegans, living according to our values is no restriction, it's a joy. Like those who don't feel restrained by not hurting, killing, or paying someone to hurt or kill a dog or a hamster, I can't feel restrained by veganism. Veganism is about abundance and inclusion. It's about living according to who we really are as human beings. Understanding that this is what the world needs—to overcome separation and violence, from and toward each other, animals and the Earth—draws me deeper into veganism. It is a wonderful thing to live my values so fully with no compromises. It is a wonderful thing that the longer I've been vegan the more I see that there are no compelling arguments against living according to the principles of nonviolence, causing fewer animals and people to suffer, and minimizing our resource use and environmental destruction.

I will always be vegan because veganism represents our attempt to take care of each other, the planet, and ourselves. I will always be vegan because it's the first fundamental step toward creating a more truthful, compassionate, and just world. I will always be vegan because it's the least that any of us can do to respect our fellow earthlings and this beautiful paradise.

Nishma Shah, Kenya/England

I am a Gujarati Indian, born into a Jain family in the coastal town of Mombasa, in Kenya. I now work as a volunteer with a group of friends as part of the Jain Vegans Working Group to raise awareness among the Jain community of how a vegan approach, rather than vegetarian (the current norm in the Jain community), is the logical way in these modern times, from so many standpoints: himsa footprint, eco footprint, health and nutrition, etc. In London, England, I also run a vegan catering and cookery class business called Shambhu's.

As a child in Mombasa, Kenya, I was brought up as a lacto-vegetarian, though our dairy consumption was very low. I have fond memories of how my mother prepared delicious meals fresh from raw, unpackaged, plant-based ingredients. My family also avoided leather items as far as possible—so no leather sofas in our house, for example. Essentially, we practised the Jain principle of respect for all life—humans, mammals, marine life, airborne life, and plant life—as far as we practically could. At the time, cow's milk was regarded as essential from a nutrition standpoint, and there was a lack of awareness as to what dairy production entailed.

It wasn't until I was in my mid-twenties and living in England, that I became aware of what dairy and leather production actually means for the mother cow and her calves. The truth was shocking, and I felt I had been lied to, or at least misled, all my childhood years. In fact, I feel that my whole family (and even the community) had been betrayed, since they too were not really aware of the truth, especially the fact that cows (at 5-8 years of age) and male calves (soon after birth) are routinely slaughtered.

I soon learned that serious man-made issues facing the world today—such as environmental destruction, loss of wildlife habitat, marine and land degradation—can all be addressed by a move away from animal-based agriculture towards a plant-based system of food production.

At the end of the day, we as human beings have the capacity to make real and practical choices that enable us to live happily, healthily and comfortably, without the need to exploit any animals whatsoever, whether for food (meat, fish, eggs, dairy, honey, etc.) or for materials (leather, fur, wool, silk, etc.). Therefore, embracing the vegan lifestyle is a complete no-brainer as I far as I'm concerned.

Geertje & Sibbelien Geertsma, the Netherlands

We, two sisters, have been living a vegan lifestyle for a year; before that we were vegetarians. Why did we choose to be vegan? It has been a process in which love and empathy have been leading the way. A few years ago our brother fell seriously ill. Obviously we were very sad and extremely involved in treating his mental situation. We wanted to be there for him completely and at the same time we felt powerless. After a while, an understanding and a feeling evolved that we could not do anything; all we could do was be there for him.

Separately we had a very special spiritual experience. It was a feeling of endless love that absorbed the ego completely. Never before had we felt so connected to the world around us and everything seemed to radiate love. Just to be there was enough and it felt like it was the right thing. Time and place did not exist anymore only a great feeling of peace. This feeling was pure and connected to all living and dying on earth. From that moment onwards, we cherish this experience and feel purity and beauty in our hearts and souls. For us, being vegan is the ultimate expression of this love. Violence and oppression do not fit in this creed.

Because we no longer accept violence to animals or use animal products, we can look all animals in the eyes and let the love flow. The parts of ourselves that hindered that do not exist anymore. We can never go back to our old ways and are very happy with our new way of life. It is a lifestyle of love for the Earth, the people, and the animals. Animals are beautiful, let them be!

Photo by El Hogar ProVegan animal sanctuary, Spain - www.elhogarprovegan.org

Anna Bonifert, Budapest, Hungary

I became vegan four years ago after reading a book called *Why vegan?* by Kath Clements. I decided instantly, mostly because of what she wrote about mother cows and their calves. As soon as I learned what happens to them, I wanted to share this knowledge with as many people as I could. This wish found the form of a blog, and a little while later regular vegan film clubs, picnics and other food tasting events where we talk about animal rights and help non-vegans make the connection and make the change.

Since the very beginning, veganism has meant a journey for me, a personal one where I can develop as an activist and it has brought me enormous joy. This has taught me a lot about faith. I used to think that humanity is hopeless, that people just don't care and that all we can do is rescue a few dogs and cats in our short little lives. But now I know that the world can change because people can change. With the environmental benefits of a vegan lifestyle there is hope for the environment as well if humanity turns vegan fast enough.

And it really is possible! Day by day I meet people who become vegan and I see how easy it is to change if the right message comes at the right time. To know this gives lots of energy. I would never go back. Never ever. Because this is the way forward. This is how we abolish slavery for good. This is how we can make sure that all animals are free to live as they feel fit. I am more than positive that peace on this planet is possible, if we go for it.

Photo provided by Karrel Christopher - www.karrelchristopher.com

Isabella La Rocca, California, USA

Being vegan is the baseline for living a compassionate, healthy, sustainable life. If humans are to survive on this planet, we must learn to live in harmony with all other earthlings. The exploitation, enslavement, and slaughter of sentient beings is a blight on our health, our environment, and our spirits. Animal agriculture is closely linked to obesity, diabetes, heart disease, and cancer. It is the single biggest contributor to groundwater, river, and ocean pollution, climate change, deforestation, and mass species extinction. Using animals for food, clothing, research, and entertainment results in a life of confinement, suffering, and torture for billions of innocent earthlings. We all deserve to be happy and free. The liberation of the most exploited among us liberates us all.

Tumeria Langlois, Massachusetts, USA

Veganism isn't a fad. It isn't something that I do to be trendy. All life matters. All life is precious. I am vegan because my life is not any more important or valuable than any other living being on the planet. I have NO need to harm another for my survival, so why would I? I listen to my heart and soul. I wish to live my life with love and compassion. All animals feel the same emotions as I do—love, joy, as well as fear. They all feel pain like I do. I don't want to be a part of their suffering. I don't want to support or have anything to do with any industry that sees living beings as mere commodities with which to make a profit. When I look into the eyes of a non-human animal, I see myself. I see a soul. I see a sentient being who only wants to live his/her life free of suffering. Humans are a part of the environment, not above it. We have no right to impose our will onto others, especially those who cannot fight back. I want to make this world a better place for all who live here. Therefore, I will always be vegan.

Laura Callas, Lake Worth, Florida, USA

I was born into a fog. That hazy, dreary fog surrounded me. Everyone around me was part of that same dark haze. So normal and right it seemed to be. I never questioned, never pondered, a non-murky life. I thought life was good, and fair, and just.

I ventured into a slightly less foggy life, for my health, that is. No meat, chicken or pork. So much better I thought. For my health, yes, for me, myself and I. I was in that semi smoggy life for a very, very long time. Yes, I was eating right for me. I loved my animal friends, and thought I was doing good. Oh, how lost I still very much was. Then one day I started to ponder, what if this wasn't enough? Was there more?

That day finally came, the haze had cleared. The sun shone down, and I could really see, crisp and clear. Oh how lost I had been all these years. I had heard a speech, and that's all it took. It made all the sense in the world to me. With the fog gone, I could see, I had been thinking only of me. Now, my heart, along with my eyes, has been opened. I see and feel the empathy, compassion, and the way to make life truly just. No harm, to ANY living being, will I be ever part of, that's a must. Once you've seen, and felt the truth, you can never go back. My heart bleeds for the innocent lives that are lost every day. I must do my part, day after day, to help clear the fog from those that surround me. So happy they will be, so many more lives to save.

Photo by C-A-L-F Sanctuary, United Kingdom

Sarah O'Toole, United Kingdom

I can state with utter certainty and sincerity that I will always remain wholeheartedly vegan. Yet, in a climate where there have been those who have made similar statements and subsequently forgone their promise of compassion towards all, that is sometimes difficult to believe. The reason I know this truth so unequivocally, is because I remember not being vegan for 33 years before I "came to". I remember what it was to be still asleep; I repeatedly awaken to the sadness of having put aside such a vital part of my consciousness. I know the ignorance that pushed wisdom to the recesses of my mind, and it serves as a reminder that I was once only partially living.

I was one of those non-vegans who genuinely thought that I knew all about compassion, but I was judgemental about vegans. I didn't understand how animals suffer, every day, in such deep and all-encompassing ways, and that to be any part of it—no matter how distantly—made me an unwitting torturer. A torturer of those who I can now honestly claim to love from the depths of my soul.

Being a mother, daughter, and wife—knowing the love of another so deeply and intensely—gave me insight into the love these other beautiful beings can feel. No matter if they are human or non-human, I do not need to be a scientist or doctor to realise that these wondrous, sentient, precious creatures can experience pain and love like I do. However, I didn't want to embrace that idea; I didn't want to see that I was hurting others unnecessarily.

Once I was brave enough to look the truth square in the eye, and to feel the grief, anger, and shame of being a party to such suffering—as well as to feel something akin to the pain these others were feeling—I was able to finally realise the truth that followed…

Being vegan has brought with it the truest joy I have ever felt besides giving birth. It is just as beautiful to give life as it is to truly honour life which exists without my interference. It is truly wonderful—and right—to deny my hand in harming others rather than denying their life or happiness itself. Just as I was originally hardwired not to harm others when I was born to life myself; and being vegan is the most alive I have ever felt!

Dunia Arcos, Barcelona, Spain

As a child I was convinced there was something wrong with me. I loved animals in a way nobody else did. I had many life companions: cats, dogs, rabbits, birds... While everybody just considered them as inferior beings, I considered they were equal to me. I strongly believed they had the same right to live than anyone of us humans. I wondered, "Why can't people understand it?"

From an early age I disliked zoos, circuses, bullfighting, barbaric festivities in which animals were abused and killed, hunting, the fur industry, even movies in which animals suffered and died. Nevertheless, as a child I was taught to eat animals and I did it for many years. I lived a dichotomy between the love I felt for animals to whom I was emotionally attached and the lack of compassion for those I consumed. I knew they were animals who suffered, but I was not brave enough to take the definite step towards true compassion. Moreover, as a child, when I cried because one of my beloved companions had passed away, my mother tried to comfort me by saying "They're only animals. They're not like us. They don't suffer the way we do." She did not comfort me though.

I remember exactly the very moment when I went vegan. It was my birthday. Previously, I had been reading some information about the dairy industry. Information on how baby calves are separated from their loving mom at birth (she is not even allowed to caress them). On how these babies die alone while their mom grieves for them. Suddenly, I felt as if I was a mother cow in a factory farm (I am not a mother though). I could feel the deep sorrow and pain she experienced when her baby was stolen from her. I determined I could not be an accomplice to that anymore.

As a vegan I have found my purpose in life: to fight for non-human rights. I have restored my inner peace. I have come to understand there is nothing wrong in loving animals. On the contrary, the wrong thing is to contribute to their exploitation and death. Veganism is not a diet, it is a way of living. The ONLY way of living rightly. That is why I will be vegan for life; for non-human persons. There is no better reason to be a vegan.

Jodi Ford, Rowley Regis, United Kingdom

"Vegan" isn't just a word to me…it's a state of life. To be vegan is to be everything I have always wanted to be. Compassionate. Thoughtful. Brave. Strong. Loving. Respectful. Protective. Nurturing. Once you've learnt how to be these things, it's impossible to go back and unlearn them. I could never again look at meat and not think of the beautiful life taken or the suffering said life endured. I could never again look at milk or eggs and not think of exploitation and cruelty. When I picture an animal, any animal, I picture them surrounded by their families and friends, at home in nature.

To me, to be a vegan is to have strong moral purpose and ingrained honour. It is to live up to my own high standards and regard all life as sacred. Whether it be a tiny ant, an Asian elephant, or anyone in between…I could no sooner stop caring for them than I could my own family. To be vegan is to link yourself to the Earth and all the creatures upon it. This link can never be severed, because I think in a way it's almost paternal. The love I have for animals and the world I live on, is the love I hope to have one day for my future children. Strong, enduring…unchanging.

I hold out hope that, soon, enough people will take a stand for what's right. I hold out hope for a future where no-one has meat on their plates, where animals are treated as equals, with the same thoughts and feelings as ourselves. I hold out hope for a world without killing, cruelty or victimisation. To be vegan is to want to make a difference. To be vegan is to want to embrace life, not throw it away. Killing costs something; it costs people a clean conscience, and animals a full, happy life. To be vegan is to want peace. Peace is, and always will be, free. That's why I will always be vegan.

Photo by Hof Butenland farmed animal sanctuary, Germany

Seyfan Lederman, Australia

When you consider the question "What is the most ethical impact we can make on the lives of animals, the environment, fellow humans, and ourselves?" veganism is the ultimate crossroad. Being vegan is a way of life that minimises harm while promoting equality, wellness and respect. In other words, veganism is an essential part of being harmonious with the Earth.

I will always be vegan because I have made the decision to stop being naïve. There is no turning back from the moment you come to the realisation that "meat" was once the muscle of a living sentient being. And from then I began to see the injustice of a massive industry born of the exploitation of animals, branching from meat to milk to eggs to leather to cosmetics, and the list doesn't just end there. How can we justify the cost?

I will always be vegan because I made the decision to stop saying "tomorrow". The most important time for activism is the present, and even one voice is strong enough to make an impact. That one voice plants a seed, and a thousand voices start a movement. I want to be a part of this "radical" shift in thinking today, in which people will come to see veganism as the norm.

I will always be vegan because I see a future of freedom. Companions do not belong on dinner plates any more. I hope that by the time I die humans will be pushed off the top of the food chain, and abattoirs and factory farms will be a thing of the past. So I will spend the rest of my years educating friends, children and strangers. That's part of the reason why I will always be vegan.

Photo by Hof Butenland farmed animal sanctuary, Germany

Marina Koltsova, Estonia

I will always be vegan because I am sharing this planet with a variety of magnificent creatures.

I will always be vegan because this is the least I can do.

I will always be vegan because I respect the rights of others even if they are disregarded by the majority.

I will always be vegan because I know everyone matters.

I will always be vegan because I have a heart and a brain and I am not afraid to use them both.

I will always be vegan because I deserve to know the truth.

I will always be vegan because I should not be forced into dominion over the powerless.

I will always be vegan because I believe in rational morality.

I will always be vegan because otherwise I would not be able to respect myself.

But most of all, I will always be vegan because there is no need for a "good reason" to not destroy someone else's life.

Photo by Daniel Henessey

Savannah Ford, PEI, Canada

I will always be vegan because when I was younger I saw a cartoon made for kids showing "happy cows" walking into one end of a building, and coming out the other as steak.

I will always be vegan because I can't look an animal in the eye and say "My ignorance is more important than your life."

I will always be vegan because animal agriculture is killing the only planet we have.

I will always be vegan because I don't see a difference between who we call pets, and who we call dinner.

I will always be vegan because I believe slavery is always wrong, no matter the species.

I will always be vegan because the animal products we kill for, are slowly killing us.

I will always be vegan because believing someone matters less than you is the root of all that's wrong with the world.

I will always be vegan because a mother's baby should never be taken from her against her will.

I will always be vegan because veganism is a moral obligation, not a simple lifestyle choice.

I will always be vegan because we should not have the right to deny others "life's simple pleasures" for our own selfish reasons.

Richard H. Schwartz, Ph.D., USA

Professor Emeritus, College of Staten Island, New York

I will always be a vegan because the vegan lifestyle is the one most consistent with Jewish (and other major religions') teachings on treating animals with compassion, preserving human health, protecting the environment, conserving natural resources, helping hungry people, and pursuing peace.

I will always be a vegan because of the widespread, horrific mistreatment of billions of animals.

I will always be a vegan because I have many pleasant ways to spend time without hunting, attending circuses or rodeos, or being involved with other activities that abuse or kill animals. I will always be a vegan because I can be comfortably and stylishly dressed without wearing clothing that involved the mistreatment of animals.

I will always be a vegan because animal-based diets contribute significantly to heart disease, several forms of cancer, strokes, and other killer diseases.

I will always be a vegan because animal-based agriculture is a major contributor to climate change, deforestation, soil erosion, deforestation, water pollution, rapid species losses, and other environmental threats to humanity.

I will always be a vegan because animal-based diets require far more land, water, energy, and other resources per person than vegan diets.

I will always be a vegan because, at a time when an estimated 20 million people worldwide die annually of hunger and its effects and almost a billion of the world's people are chronically hungry, 70 percent of the grain produced in the United States is fed to animals destined for slaughter.

I will always be a vegan because in an increasingly thirsty world, with glaciers melting, aquifers shrinking, and lakes drying, it takes up to 14 times as much water for a person on an animal-based diet than for a person on a plant-based diet.

I will always be a vegan because it is my way to protest against the "madness and sheer insanity" that animal-based diets represent.

I will always be a vegan because it is arguably the most important thing I can do for my health, animals, the environment, the efficient use of natural resources, hungry people, and efforts toward a more peaceful, just world.

I will always be a vegan because only if many people become vegans will we have a chance to help shift our imperiled planet onto a sustainable path.

Gope Suresh, Zhejiang Province, China

Indian, living in China for over a decade, but considers self an 'earthling'

I was vegetarian for 27 years, had strong will power; life was nice to me. There were questions within.

I became non-veg for 10 years, had fears, worries, agitation, frustrations, and ignorance, even though I did not relish the non-veg that I ate once a week.

At age 41, I became vegan all of sudden, after witnessing the killing of fish on the road by a restaurant, though without knowing about veganism. There was always a voice within, as most humans have, but generally parents, guardians, elders, and friends push us to forget; ignore it as a sign of non-conformity with man-made society. After going vegan, I regained my positive thought attraction, strong will power, ability to focus on my vision, found compassion and empathy for others, as well as maintained health without exercise.

I have found the power within to be simple, to create positive events, to be the change within, to align with nature, to trust, and to have faith in the universe through the vegan way. I hope to unite with dignity to face questions (if any) until my last day of this human form.

So I hope, pray, wish, desire, and seek powers, contacts, and associations, to see harmony between sentient beings and to understand the purpose of the universe's plan; not the man-made plan of growing the economy by destroying nature for future generations.

I did not know the whole man-made system of education, health, fashion, entertainment, and economy is based on the abuse of animals. I have stopped buying wool, silk, and animal-tested cosmetics for my family, and I do not intend or dream of doing it again, even in worst case scenarios.

I have traveled 25 countries; most divided by color, race, religion, and region, but found vegans (not for health) uniting the world and giving hope, peace, and harmony to the world. Thanks to all of them.

Paul Stevenson, Northland, New Zealand

I am vegan because it is the kind thing to do. I like the Golden Rule, "Do unto others as you would have them do unto you." I include members of other species as "others" because they have feelings just like us, experience the world like us and suffer as we do.

Kindness is central to the Golden Rule. Kindness is an essential part of justice, and justice of progress. Without kindness there is no justice, no happiness and no progress. The Golden Rule therefore obligates us to be vegan because there is no alternative.

The entire animal industry, including the use of animals for food, fabrics, research and entertainment, is monstrously brutal. Suffering is integral to it; it requires suffering. Anyone supporting the animal industry is therefore directly responsible for causing immense suffering. It is despicable that we should require others to suffer to satisfy our pleasure when there are alternatives that cause no suffering. We cannot live by the Golden Rule if we support this industry. This is why I will always be vegan.

There is more to kindness than at first meets the eye. It has consequences for both parties; giver and receiver. Treating others unkindly is a lose-lose situation. The victims of our unkindness are harmed by it, but so are we. To be unkind is to act beneath ourselves. As a result we lose hugely. Unkindness degrades us and destroys our dignity. When we casually cause and ignore the suffering of others we become pathetic people indeed; we become small, hard and mean—ignoble. In the end we lose our humanity itself, the very essence of what it is to be human.

By contrast, being kind to others is a win-win situation. The recipients of kindness benefit from it, but the person who performs the kindness gains immensely. We feel elevated; we become bigger, happier people. Paradoxically, we gain even when we apparently lose, when donating blood for example. Kindness elevates and ennobles us. Kindness bestows undreamt of joy upon us. Our hearts glow. Only by being kind to others can we know true happiness. There can be no justice, no joy without kindness. In rejecting cruelty and adopting a life based on kindness we regain and expand our humanity. That makes the world a better place for all.

Johneh Zha Sankar, Chennai, India

I will always be vegan because I am grateful for this human life and all the privileges that nature (LIFE) has given me. I believe I am instructed to take dominion over the creatures of Earth, which means I should take care of their well-being; I should not harm them for any reason.

I will never go back to an omnivorous, non-humane diet or lifestyle; as it attaches more sin and negative karma to my aura. It's not just that I want to save the planet or environment. After all I am too small to save such a big system. I am just saving myself. I shall be humble in front of the planet Earth, as I am just a nomadic soul staying under its shade for a short while. Being pragmatic, a vegan diet keeps me alive, with energy rather than just surviving. I am conscious. The uncomplicated decency of every human is to live cruelty-free. As Noah says, real strength comes from the creator, not from flesh.

As a vegan, and a part of a big vegan family around the world, I am moving a block against the whole mess created by humanity for all these millennia. So there's no possibility of giving up in this fight. We have ruined the planet, and the only way to heal the wounds is to go vegan, embrace nature and live humanely. It might seem difficult, but I believe it is more than just possible.

"Vitamin deficiency" they will say. "Immune deficiency" they will say. Those people with eyes closed and mouth wide open; they will say anything to pull you back to the crowd. However, as a vegan for 4+ years, I've ditched those myths. Many have. I get sufficient vitamins and protein just as a rhinoceros does. Even if I am facing a deficiency, I will always search for a cruelty-free alternative for getting my needs fulfilled. People on omnivorous diets get more diseases and deficiencies than vegans. So there's no SPECIAL DEAL killing and exploiting fellow earthlings.

To live is to let others live too. I've opened my eyes to conscious and grateful living, and I will not close my eyes until I turn cold. Go vegan, stay vegan, so we can save ourselves from endless miseries. I will always be a vegan, for my entire life.

Dr. Andy Mars, Ph.D., California, USA

I will always be vegan for the same reasons that I went vegan decades ago in the first place. It was the right thing to do then, it is the right thing to do now, and it will always be the right thing to do. Right exists beyond you and me. Right is not a matter of opinion or perspective. Most of what is right can be clearly seen by stepping back from one's own personal situation and looking at the big picture beyond any one of us. From an ethical, environmental, and any other unselfish standpoint, being vegan is the right thing to do.

Why will I always be vegan? Why will I always be conscious and compassionate? Why will I always use the mind and heart with which I am blessed? My heart feels for others, and my mind thinks of others. I look beyond my own eyes, and I see the benefit to the others with whom I share this planet and to the planet itself. I will always be vegan because I am focused on what is right beyond my own personal existence. There is absolutely no need and no reasonable justification for us to use other animals for our own purposes. I do not want to be responsible for taking the life of, or causing harm in any way to, other animals. Every life should have the right to exist for its own purpose and meaning, and not for someone else's.

My life is not just about me. Someday I will be dead and gone. What I ate, what I wore, what I bought, what I enjoyed as entertainment, none of this will matter for me when I am dead and gone. It will, however, matter if I made such choices at the expense of others. There is no good reason for me to cause harm to others. Whether or not there is a life that awaits us after this existence, whether or not we will ultimately be judged, whether or not rewards await, whether or not there are punishments to avoid, being vegan is the right way to live here and now. That is why I went vegan, that is why I am vegan, and this is why I will always be vegan. Being vegan is the ideal way, the right way, to live.

Dr. Andy Mars and K9

Michael Lanfield, Toronto, Canada

Author of 'The Interconnectedness of Life'

As I look back at the first 26 years of my life, I was simply forced by our culture, my parents and all institutions to consume animal foods. It was nothing of my own doing, and as the years went by I never thought for a second about the effect my food choices had on animals and the Earth. Since becoming vegan in 2009 and advocating on behalf of all animals, I have decided to dedicate my life to helping them. The animals have inspired me to continue the fight on their behalf against their enslavement and use. If it weren't for them, I would have no reason to be living today.

A few years later, I started bearing witness to pigs and cows transported to slaughter. I was horrified, but at the same time saddened for the animals. As we looked into each other's eyes, they knew they were going to slaughter; they pleaded and begged for mercy. They saw their brothers and sisters in front of them going to their deaths. They are not stupid animals. In my 32 years on this planet, I have never been so heartbroken and yet so alive and joyful knowing that I'm helping thousands of animals, humans and the interconnected web of life with my buying choices and eating habits.

Animals taught me to unconditionally love everyone and to share that message with others. They've inspired me to continue the work, writing and spreading their voice wherever I go. I'm very proud in knowing, that with every meal, I am contributing to a kinder and more just world for everyone. Being vegan is the greatest step we can take to preserve the environment and be healthy but, most important, we know it's the right thing to do for the defenseless animals that we gluttonously devour at every meal. One day we'll look back and see how barbaric we were forcing cruelty upon animals and destroying nature around us. May all beings live free to roam the prairies, plains and waters of the Earth.

Lukas Cech, Slovakia

I will always be vegan, because it is the only way to have a clear conscience, to fall asleep happy at night. Knowing what I know, it is the worst crime to continue to support cruel businesses, just because it is convenient.

I will always be vegan, because if I do not do something, no one else will do it for me. I want to be the change I want to see in the world; live by the words of Gandhi. I want to show other people that a compassionate lifestyle is not difficult and is the way forward.

I will always be vegan, because I have the words, actions and influence to make a difference. Animals do not. They are the innocent creatures suffering for our gluttony and luxury, but the world is ignorant to their cries. I want to be their voice.

I will always be vegan, because I feel I owe it to all the suffering creatures all around the world. Even if in today's society there are places where it is still not as easy to be vegan as in other places, this little "inconvenience" is nothing compared to the suffering the animals go through.

I will always be vegan, because I do not feel that animals are mine to control, enslave, or use for my own benefit, or to please my taste.

I will always be vegan, because most of the pain animals go through is caused by humans and they have no way to defend themselves.

Drawing by Jo Frederiks - www.jofrederiks.com

Rune Kjær Rasmussen, Odense, Denmark

I have a T-shirt that says "I am vegan because I love life". That is how simple it really is to me. I deeply love the idea that I can live as respectful as possible by being vegan. I think of it as releasing as much empathy into every corner of life as possible. Veganism is common sense waiting to be common; because to not contribute to the suffering and death of others is common sense. I have my senses as a human. Everyone who is not human has theirs. Their lives are without a doubt as invaluably interesting an experience as mine. To become vegan is to acknowledge that the arrogance of demanding a human template for non-human life in order to deem it worthy is a kind of madness that will perhaps mean that humans will self-destruct and kill so many other species while doing so.

However I have real hope that the opposite will happen, because I see it. Many people try in various ways to make that change. And I think many people will understand that message because it is a message of hope. We as humans are not outside of nature because nothing and nobody is outside of nature. And nature wants to celebrate life. That is very obvious when one can see it. Veganism is a very important thread in that celebration. And it is based on rights that everyone should be born with: rights for nature to be nature. The artificial human-made hierarchy threatening to destroy so much should be replaced by equality in every possible way. We are here right now. Let us enjoy it and let others enjoy it as well. Love life!

Photo provided by Karrel Christopher - www.karrelchristopher.com

66

Trang Ly, Vietnam

There are three reasons why I will always be vegan. Firstly, I deeply believe that all animals experience pain, and feelings such as happiness and fear. They also love their lives and their children, and nobody wants to be someone else's meal. In addition, I suppose animals are like our younger sisters or brothers. Unfortunately, they cannot speak up to protect themselves, but if they could use the language of humans, they would ask us to be vegan to save their precious lives. They are not our food, nor entertainment, and should not be taken advantage of for clothing, testing or other purposes. Therefore, I chose the vegan lifestyle more than seven years ago because from the bottom of my heart I think harming sentient beings is a cruel action.

Secondly, veganism helped me see more clearly with regard to many issues which I did not know how to tackle. I have heard people say things like "You're as stupid as a cow or a pig" when they got angry with someone. However, they eat beef or pork to get nutrition and drink cow's milk to get strong bones. I always wonder why people who think that we're the most intelligent species on the planet keep making these foolish choices. It seems most non-vegans do not care much about what or whom they are consuming or exploiting.

Here is a Vietnamese story which I've read on Facebook. One day, a calf asked his mother "Mommy, where will I be after I die?" "Our relatives will be buried in meat eaters' stomachs, dear!" The mother cow replied sadly to her child. Like the above story, a long thoughtful sentence that is repeated many times in daily conversation in my hometown to remind non-vegans is: "Their abdomens are surely an animal cemetery where countless dead animal bodies were buried." This horrible thought may disgust you, but it is the truth that may not be easy to perceive if you are not a vegan.

Lastly, I could say that I will forever maintain veganism since I really love a harmonious atmosphere, therefore I cannot go in the same direction as the vicious crowd. Harmony and peace in the world can be achieved if each individual senses real peace in their mind.

Jennifer Nitz, USA

Graduating 8th grade should have been one of the happiest times of my life. Instead, my best friend died and I was heartbroken. She was a basset hound named Sadie. I had a connection with her that I could never put into words, until I saw the posters of a dog and pig that read, "Why love one and eat the other?" I became a vegetarian after she died. Then in 1994, my junior year in college, I took an Animal Behavior course and we took a field trip to study abnormal behavior in farm animals. I saw the female cows lined up with their heads barricaded into their feed while their teets were being suctioned by machines. The cows that weren't in that situation were in the front of the barn crowded and jumping on each other. I was disgusted and decided "I am not contributing to this", and stopped consuming dairy that day. I didn't know there was a word "vegan", or dairy substitutes, and didn't care. I never missed it either. I just knew I wasn't contributing to the poor treatment of animals like those I saw in that barn, or eating animals that I knew had the same feelings that my best friend Sadie had.

I was a typical city girl who grew up minutes from Chicago. I didn't know any other vegetarians, just that I could not eat another animal, or after that college course, consume dairy. I then moved out west and met environmental and animal rights activists, and learned many more reasons to be vegan (a new word too!). I couldn't understand why so many of these activists weren't vegan knowing what they knew, while I was just learning! I went to Buffalo Nations and found out why the native wild buffalo were being slaughtered. The livestock industry was lead agency in the slaughter, and many of those activists weren't vegan, huh? I went to work at a farm sanctuary and found out veal was a direct product of the dairy industry, and saw what "free range" and "cage free" meant. I couldn't understand why everyone I talked to about it didn't immediately go vegan. I learned about the air and water pollution, and the land consumption it takes to raise the animals, and remember dear Sadie, who I see in all other animals' eyes. This is all why I will never stop speaking up for the rights of all animals, and of course, why I will always be vegan!

Alicia Lim, Singapore

I did not grow up vegan. Like most people, I was socialized into believing that it was natural and our right to eat animals and use animal products. They were just things I enjoyed, pieces of food, leather shoes.

The dog friends I was blessed to know taught me otherwise. I saw how they felt love, joy, desire, how they suffered from fear, illnesses, pain. It gradually became clear to me that they were fundamentally no different from the other animals we use, and if they had feelings, the animals we eat and wear must have them too.

I thought about the fish swimming placidly in tanks at restaurants, hauled up and chopped to death for a customer. I thought about the bored, lonely, depressed-looking animals imprisoned in zoos for our entertainment. And the cute, innocent lamb I cuddled and the fluffy, woolly sheep at a farm I visited, and the violent death in store for them that I never thought about while there. I learned that veal comes from the dairy industry, that male baby calves and male chicks are killed, that their mothers, who can never love their children, are also killed when they no longer produce enough, so that I could have dairy and eggs. The suffering we put animals through to fulfill our various human wants is a horror deliberately kept hidden from our eyes, the worst nightmare we would never want ourselves or our loved ones to experience.

I was attached to the taste of animal products and reluctant to give them up, but becoming vegan made me happy and at peace with myself. I was finally doing what I knew was right, and stopping what I knew was wrong. Now I look at leather, wool, pieces of meat, and I see the animals who struggled desperately in fear and pain for their lives.

I will always be vegan because I cannot ever again, in any way, justify supporting harm to others who want to avoid suffering, enjoy their meals, and live their days in peace. Those are basic desires of humans, and all other animals desire the same. We are perfectly able to live well without using them, so how can we justify choosing to do otherwise? Animals are not things, they are feeling beings with the capacity for love and pain, whose lives are their own, never ours to use.

Dominika Piasecka, Poland

I will always be vegan because I have a choice: I choose compassion over cruelty. I don't want to be a person who is content with how things are. I want to be heard, be different, create change. We can make the world a better place, where all beings are equal, as it should be. Being vegan really is the least one can do, and when you look at what billions of innocent animals are going through every second of every day, it doesn't seem difficult at all.

I always say everyone has a mission in their life; you just need to find out what it is. Mine is to fight for animals exploited for food; used for clothing, entertainment, in experiments; or abused in any other way. No one deserves to suffer, especially those somehow "weaker" than us—those without a voice.

People don't want to hear the truth because they don't want their illusions destroyed. It's so much easier to stay ignorant and selfish, isn't it? Life's most persistent question is, "What are you doing for others?" If you're not giving the world the best you have, what world are you saving it for? People may doubt what you say, but they will believe what you do. This is my motivation to never to stop screaming my heart out for what I am passionate about and getting involved in animal rights. Veganism is a part of me I can't live without, just like my heart or my head. It's what I'm most proud of about myself and I want the world to know that. I've dedicated my life to saving animals and I'm perfectly happy with it.

They say one vegan won't make a difference, but I know I do make a difference every single day. Desmond Tutu said, "Do your little bit of good where you are; it's those little bits of good put together that overwhelm the world." And this is why I never doubt that a small group of dedicated, passionate people can change the world. Of course not everyone understands why I do this. But that's okay. One day they will. One day they will look back and wish they'd been doing the same.

One day the animals will all be free, in a world without cages.

Lisa Colvin, Salado, Texas, USA

The lamb's leg,
The cow's skin,
The pig's rib,
The chicken's thigh,
The turkey's breast,
The cow's milk,
The crab's claw,
And the deer's horn.

They are not mine.
They belong to the animals.

Just as
The llama's leg,
The dog's skin,
The cat's rib,
The eagle's thigh,
The robin's breast,
The horse's milk,
The parrot's claw,
And the giraffe's horn
Belong to them.
Why is one more deserving of protection than the other?

Speciesism,
So clearly unjust and immoral.

Each animal's right is to live in peace
Enjoying life on Earth
As a "who" and a "him" and a "her",
Not as an "it"
In a store freezer,
Or in an oven,
Or on a menu.
Not as entertainment,
Or furniture,
Or clothing,
Or accessories.

Animals,
All animals,
Are extraordinary gifts,
Each beautiful and unique,
Precious
Innocent
Sensitive
Intelligent
Social
And trusting.

Trusting of humans,
But heartbroken by humans,
And betrayed by humans.

Veganism
Is the opposite of
Speciesism.

It is how I choose to live.
I imagine the day when
All animals
Are valued by humans,
Protected by humans,
Respected by humans,
Connected with humans.

Photo by Hof Butenland farmed animal sanctuary, Germany

Madhur Patel, Switzerland

I grew up in a Jain vegetarian family in India. Although we did not have any pets at home, compassion and Ahimsa (non-violence) towards animals, including minute insects, was part of our lifestyle. I consumed dairy for about 25 years of my life thinking there was no cruelty in the dairy industry, at least not in India where Hindus sometimes worship cows. Moreover, in Switzerland it is very easy to spot cows grazing happily.

I am a truth seeker. I started educating myself about veganism and I watched the documentary *Earthlings*. It was a life changing experience! You can watch it for free online. After that I drastically reduced my dairy consumption.

In 2011, I visited a small dairy farm in Switzerland as part of a project to educate kids (aged 9-13) about the ecological footprint of different foods. We played creative games to educate the children. While we were educating them, a herd of cows walked past us. One of the cows had an enormous udder. She was suffering from mastitis— inflammation of the udder caused by using milking machines multiple times a day to suck the udders dry. All the kids started laughing boisterously upon seeing the cow. I was disappointed and felt sorry for the cow. It was an aha-moment! Those kids had already been brainwashed by society to view animals as commodities for human use. No beverage on this planet is worth the suffering that it causes to these animals.

I used that opportunity to interview the farmer about the dairy industry, which I had learned about in the past by watching videos and reading about animals and food production. It confirmed what I already knew. That evening, after coming back home, I watched a speech on YouTube and it was the final push to go vegan. I have been an (ethical) vegan ever since and it is one of the best things I have ever done in my life!

I often meet people who think being vegan is so difficult. I say if you go vegan for the animals, it is the easiest thing in the world. It makes you healthier, reduces your carbon footprint, and most importantly it causes the least harm to animals. Isn't that a perfect win-win situation?

Madeleine Lifsey, USA

Chair, *Animal Advocates of Smith College*

Around age 13, I began learning more about factory farming. Though I had been vegetarian for years, I was just beginning to fully grasp the connection between the animals themselves, who I did not want to hurt, and the "products" that I was consuming that came into my life only through direct exploitation. Through articles, undercover video footage, interviews, and books, I learned that all systems of oppression are interconnected. I learned that mothers do cry when their calves are taken away, and that billions of birds live their entire lives without once seeing sunlight or feeling grass. What startled me most was learning the fate of male chicks. The industry I was supporting literally threw living babies away as garbage because of their sex. Learning this solidified my already growing resolve that I no longer wanted any part of it.

Upon graduating high school, I had the privilege of spending a few months living and volunteering at a vegan-run animal sanctuary. Though I was already vegan, my time at the sanctuary gave me a rare window into the lives and personalities of the survivors of the industry that I had vehemently opposed for so long. One with whom I developed a particularly close friendship was Petunia, a then two-week-old piglet who had been discarded because she was small. She would have been left for dead because her body was not considered profitable, but with surgery and patient care at the sanctuary, she bounced back to thrive as a friendly, curious, and wildly intelligent youngster.

Years before, I had decided that there was already plenty of suffering in the world without my adding any more to the mix. Looking into Petunia's eyes, I saw a dignified individual, never an object to be consumed. She was one of the lucky survivors, but when I see any animal's body on a plate today, that animal is no less "somebody" than she was when she was alive. That realization is an integral part of my being, and I cannot imagine existing any other way. You don't need to be an "animal lover" to be vegan, just as you don't need to love kids in order not to take part in child abuse. All we need is to develop an awareness of the acute suffering being inflicted upon hundreds of billions of innocents around the world, and make the conscious choice to stop taking part.

Лана Смолина (Lana Smolina), **Ukraine**

I am vegan because I want to live fully in peace without causing any pain or bloodshed. I believe all the animals and people suffering do not disappear; they accumulate somewhere to come back to us again. Being vegan, I believe that I reduce the amount of suffering in this world. I hope that my vegan living shows people the right way to live life, full of love and kindness.

Jenny Johansson, **Sweden**

When I became vegan, it felt like I had truly awakened and evolved as a human being; a compassionate one. I will always be vegan because I believe in a world where animals live free and in harmony with humans. A world where we as humans have rid ourselves of old habits and cruel traditions, where there is no more starvation and no suffering; a clean, cruelty free world for all of Earth's inhabitants.

Photo by C-A-L-F Sanctuary, United Kingdom

Ana-Maria Stefania, Nicosia, Cyprus

Looking back in my life, counting my achievements in degrees, recognitions or distinctions, my greatest achievement is becoming vegan. That is my greatest award; my pride in being a real human!

Absolutely nothing can go above or beyond the significance of the moment when I pressed the "play" button on a video called *Earthlings*. That moment was my "birthday", for that was the moment I started to finally live and not merely exist.

Veganism is about real living, feeling, sensing, seeing, hearing, and smelling. It is about testing and experiencing true freedom, knowledge and intelligence at its finest. Veganism is about knowing what a marvellous creation life is, and not living off of others' pain, suffering, and enslavement.

The moment I understood ALL BEINGS are interconnected, was the moment I released myself from the prison of being controlled by fear and limitations. That was the moment I started to reverse the "brain-washing" that has been imposed for millennia through religions, education systems, and the food and medical industries.

What converts people into "real humans" is their own thoughts and actions towards their fellow co-inhabitants of this wonderful planet. Real humans treat every being with respect and never intentionally cause any form of harm.

I will always be vegan because I see in every animal, in every being, a marvellous creation willing to live, enjoy life and the whole process of evolution. I deeply understand that I have no right to force animals to live in cage-prisons or to be raped and bred, or to deprive them of light, of fresh air, of creating lifetime friendships, and of freedom. Why do I have to pay someone else to do such crimes on my behalf? Is it fair or just? Is it necessary? No, definitely no!

All people talk about Peace on Earth. Can we really talk about peace with a mouth full of blood? My journey on Earth as a vegan is about making our planet a better place, living in peace and harmony with ALL BEINGS, regardless of species, race, religion, or sexual orientation. Veganism is the way to end worldwide poverty and live abundantly and joyous! Veganism is about saving our Earth from the harm that we all have contributed to, for so long. I am here to add my little contribution along with millions of awakened humans working towards a planet where ALL forms of life are respected and appreciated.

Let's make our Mother Earth what she was meant to be! All together, united, with kindness towards ALL BEINGS!

Anke Hagen, Hanover, North Germany

I grew up in South Africa and experienced a number of transformative, life-changing events at an early receptive age, like trying to bargain with a female witch doctor who worked for my parents when she wanted to slaughter some chickens in our garden, "who" she had "procured" for her magic. The chickens were afraid and one of them had escaped onto the roof of a tool shed in the back garden. I offered my blood instead and even slit my forearm dramatically to convince her that I could provide an adequate substitute on the spot, but she wasn't interested because the blood had to be from a chicken.

It culminated in an immediate decision to give up eating non-human animal body parts when I witnessed the slaughter of a lamb that had been happily prancing around across the road from my father's factory. The workers grabbed him, took him to the factory premises and slaughtered him on the concrete floor of the factory compound, directly in front of me. From one moment to the next this poor creature's abdominal contents were being removed, and then I smelled his flesh being barbecued. The transition from life, vitality, to this familiar smell was horrifically fast! It was surreal and I was sickened to the core! I became a vegetarian on the spot and was severely traumatized, despite my mother's protests that she wasn't going to allow me to "mess up the order in her kitchen". I was 14. Ironically, my father had given me a toy lamb when I was a young child that looked quite similar to the lamb that had just been slaughtered on his factory premises. That seems quite symbolic in retrospect.

It is only when I saw all the postings on Facebook that explained why it was hypocritical to continue to consume animal products and ethically necessary to go vegan that I was forced to grapple with the gaps in my logic. I realized that—ethically speaking—I had been lulled into a sense of complacency about the amount I had been doing as a vegetarian all those years, and that it was now time to wake up completely!

I went vegan in 2013 and it was one of the very best decisions I have made in my life! It was also extremely easy and I literally feel like the person in the film *The Matrix* who was offered the choice of the blue or red pill: totally transformed in a way that even living as a vegetarian cannot achieve! It goes without saying that I will never reconsider my decision. I finally feel as though I have found my way "home".

Jenny Chambers, United Kingdom

Everyone has a theory on how the world came to be, but there's no definitive answer and there probably never will be. For me, the only thing that matters is that the world did come to be and here we all are; breathing, communicating, living. You may assume I am referring to the human race, but in actual fact I am referring to all living beings; human or otherwise. Don't we all breathe? Don't we all communicate? Don't we all live? There is a strong sense of superiority amongst the members of the human race and, to put it bluntly, I find this infuriating. I understand the arguments for it; we can build houses that last a lifetime, design and engineer machines to do pretty much anything we want, and we even have enough power to use any other species to benefit ourselves in any way we like. However, some of the attributes that make the human race great are also the things that can make us somewhat heartless.

We live in a world where greed prevails and compassion seems to be disregarded. Those high rise buildings don't mean everyone will have a safe place to sleep. We created machines that can kill thousands within seconds, and just because we can overpower other living beings doesn't mean we should. So when taking this into account, I still see no reason why we should consider ourselves more important than any other species. Every living being deserves the chance to live. Not just exist, but to live a life free of cruelty, torture or captivity, the same as any human deserves.

Sometimes it seems like my heart can break a million times every day. It can be a passerby munching on a bacon sandwich, a pop-up on Facebook advertising the local zoo, or a billboard claiming to have the best tasting milk. While most people would see a delicious lunch, an enjoyable Saturday afternoon, or the thirst quenching white stuff, I see it all differently. This is not a choice I consciously make, it just happens; I see the terrified pig in the slaughter-house; a lonely lifetime of suffering in front of a crowd; the calf who was callously taken away from his/her mother.

These are just a few reasons why I will always be vegan.

Lyra Alves, Belgium

Brazilian living in Belgium for 15 years

I was brought up in a very carnivorous environment in Brazil. My father strictly made sure my brother and I ate all kinds of foods. I remember my brother crying, looking at his food on the table, saying that the chicken on his plate was his friend and now she was dead. He was forced to eat her anyway. At a certain age, I had learned to enjoy animal foods and ate lots of dead barbecued bodies. They told me we humans need meat to survive and be healthy. I was also told at school, that if we did not eat animals they would take over the entire planet. By eating them I was in fact helping to restore the natural balance.

I was 16 when I met this amazing and independent woman who told me she had quit eating meat and felt so much better. Her thoughts were clearer, her emotions more stable, and she felt more energetic than ever. I was always very interested in mind-improving things so I decided to give it a try to see if I felt what she meant. Call it being impressionable, but at 16 we are indeed trying out various paths in life. So I tried not eating meat for a month and I can't explain what happened but I just could never go back to eating any dead corpse. My view of the world had totally changed, even though I could not say why exactly.

A year later I went to a lecture by a spiritual philosopher who gave inspiring talks. He would speak about things I had never heard anywhere else, but somehow they totally made sense to me. One of his ideas was that if humans were the most evolved beings on the planet, it was our responsibility to engage in higher ethical behaviours. That would include compassion and respect for all living creatures. He talked about the absurdity of taking the lives of sentient beings and torturing them for their products, when we do not even need them. I realised how barbaric my entire education had been; both at home and at school. Since then I see animals no longer as products, but as co-earthlings. I've been vegan for 25 years. Once we open our minds and hearts to this reality, there is just no going back.

Sharon LeMay, Minnesota, USA

The well known cliché states: Once you know, you can never forget. Yet, many vegans do forget, as knowledge becomes inconvenient, problematic, or simply gets between them and a coveted hamburger. This essay is about why I'll never forget, and vow to remain vegan forever.

In the grand scheme of things, it's easy to think one person makes no difference. In my lifetime, how many cows will be saved by my not eating them; how many shampoos not sold because they are not cruelty free and vegan so I won't buy them? And the answer is: not many. Out of the millions of animal based products produced each day, my non-participation is barely going to make a dent in the machine. It is easy to see how some look at this scenario and figure one little scone made with heavy cream isn't going to matter—I'll cheat this once. Those cheats then grow in number as the person makes this excuse and that, until they are vegan no more. I will suggest this is the wrong way to look at things. To think we are too insignificant to matter is the timeworn strategy used against people to quell dissent and we need to be aware of its use against vegans. We need to realize that everything starts with one and then grows. And in our lives, that one is us. And eventually, one by one by one, we will be powerful enough to effect change.

I live daily with this knowledge. Both the knowledge of the horrors involved in using animals for food, clothing, entertainment, testing, and pleasure, and the knowledge that just one person can make at least some difference. I read a story once which remains imprinted in my mind: A little boy is walking along a seashore strewn with beached starfish which are slowly dying. He walks along and throws them back into the sea. He throws back as many as he can, but there are too many to save them all. A man approaches and asks, "Why bother? There are just too many to save. You can't make any difference." The little boy bends over and picks up another starfish and flings it into the sea and says, "I just made a difference to that one." This is why I'll never cease being vegan. Every day, no matter how large or small, my choices matter.

Andrew Begg, Bucharest, Romania

I will always be vegan because the thought of causing harm to an animal is anathema to me. It goes against everything I stand for. I am interested in fundamental justice and treating everyone equally and with respect. I stand up for the innocent and vulnerable and there is no group more helpless and deserving of our kindness, mercy, and protection than animals. By definition, that means being vegan. I could do more for animals and sometimes I do, but for me my veganism is a baseline minimum, and it is constant. Its consistent principles of compassion and kindness light my path through life.

Animals are my friends, and some of the best friends I've had throughout my life have been animals. I have always loved their presence, and there are many occasions when I prefer the company of animals to humans. Therefore it is logical to be vegan; there is simply no alternative, not that I would want there to be. I wouldn't hurt a human friend, so why would I consider hurting an animal friend? They are one and the same, and the thought of hurting either is equally repellent.

I like setting an example, and try to be a good influence in people's lives. I engage as many people as I can in discussion on the subject of veganism and animal rights, and find that people are genuinely interested and want to know more. I find they want to do good, want to do what is right, but often don't know how. I never back out of a conversation or miss an opportunity, because I know I'm in the right. Whoever said there is no argument against veganism is spot-on.

Every time I see a vegan friend, she remarks on how good it is to be vegan. I feel the same. Being involved in a movement whose principles are founded on compassion, peace, and kindness is wonderful. I want to do whatever I can to see the movement develop into the mainstream.

Like every vegan I've met, I just wish I'd discovered veganism earlier, but coming from an animal abusing background somehow makes its renunciation all the more gratifying. Having discovered the best way to live, the best way to be, I'll stick with it for the rest of my days.

Dr. C. Michele Martindill, New Mexico, USA

Why I Will Always be Vegan – My Practice of Ahimsa

I came to veganism through the concept of Ahimsa: nonviolence toward self and others. My first encounter with the Sanskrit term came when I was studying philosophy and religion as an undergraduate in the early 1970s. As an anti-war activist and pacifist, my focus was on social justice issues, but it was not until I was working at a kill shelter in the late 1980s that I was introduced to veganism. Vegan volunteers at the shelter blamed shelter employees for the cruelty we inflicted on dogs and cats on a daily basis, and these vegans—upper class white women—showed little compassion for the workers who lacked education to work elsewhere and were just doing the best they could to survive. I was writing my Master's thesis on how kill shelters were a dumping ground for unwanted animals, and I could not identify with these vegans who practiced blatant classism.

By the early 1990s my practice of yoga and Ahimsa gradually brought me to understand that there was violence on my dinner plate, and I did not want to consume violence. Still, I resisted the "vegan" label. I have no specific date for when I started saying I was vegan. To be clear, I do not see veganism as a diet. Veganism means compassion toward all living beings, and working to end all oppression and exploitation of others. Veganism stands opposed to racism, sexism, ageism, ableism, classism and speciesism.

I often question the meaning of veganism and my involvement with the movement. So many vegans tell people to just "go vegan", and that the liberation of other animals will lead to the liberation of all living beings. I wish it could be so simple. It is no surprise that some vegans want to limit the scope of veganism, having it refer to just the animals, especially since the movement has a white upper class male-dominated leadership, is comprised mostly of white women followers, and shows little interest in addressing human oppression. It is a challenge to identify with a movement more concerned about the latest vegan products on the market than with the child slave labor that produces most of the cocoa used in the world. My lifetime commitment to veganism is the strongest action I can take to end all oppression.

Rohana Norgate, **Melbourne, Australia**

At the age of four I made the connection between the meat on my plate and my beloved animal friends. Much to my parents' dismay, meal times became a battle for many years. "I will not eat my friends!" I would say. By the age of 11, I was vegetarian and had finally gained my family's support. At 16 my Grandmother said "This isn't just a phase is it, dear?" During my teenage years I started writing to cosmetic companies asking if they tested their products on animals. When the reply said "yes" I would write another long letter explaining my disgust and vowing to never buy their brand again.

By the time I was in my mid 20s the internet was very accessible and I started to discover the awful truths about the leather, egg and dairy industries. I must admit, of all things, I found cheese difficult to give up. That is until one day when I was in a small country town on my way home from holiday. We were filling up the car when a ute pulled up; it was pulling a trailer filled with small terrified baby calves, their sweet faces were full of fright and confusion. Tears sprang to my eyes. Must these creatures suffer just for us to enjoy a moment of having them on our plates or for a macabre fashion statement? I vowed to be vegan from that day on.

I no longer think of my lifestyle and diet as restrictive or a sacrifice, I feel liberated! I feel healthy and I feel full of love. For the rest of my life I will be spreading the vegan word, for our bodies, for our planet, for our souls, but mostly for our fellow earthlings.

Photo by C-A-L-F Sanctuary, United Kingdom

Ines Hoefling, Germany

I will always be vegan, because to me being vegan isn't a lifestyle as many people consider it to be. It might be a trend at the moment to eat vegan in order to maintain a healthy lifestyle, or to help fight ecological problems that have occurred in the course of the past decades. It might be convenient because store shelves seem to burst over with plant-based products (so I would say it is a nice side effect to be able to access alternative products so easily). But being vegan is more than that.

Just as people in the past fought slavery because it was simply unjust, or people tried to achieve equal rights for women, today we have to stand up and raise our voices for animals who can't speak for themselves. We can raise our voices and make an effort by boycotting animal derived products, be it food, leather and fur, or cosmetics tested on animals. They're not ours to use. They're not objects, but sentient living beings. If I got the chance to ask somebody who lived in the 18th century why they were treating black people in such a bad way, they would have told me it's because they're a different color, therefore worth less, and that this is just the way it is.

Today, most people's excuse not to include animals in their morals is that they're from a different species. Isn't the species argument just as random as the color argument used to be? I think it is. So if awareness rises and one day change comes, and our grandchildren or their grandchildren get the chance to ask us: "Why did you treat animals the way you used to?" What would you tell them? At least I know I wouldn't have to admit that I have been part of the cruelty in today's world. Compassion is one of the most important emotional components human beings have. Why do we make such little use of it?

Photo by El Hogar ProVegan animal sanctuary, Spain - www.elhogarprovegan.org 84

Sandra Shama Kaur, Cairo, Egypt

I come from an Egyptian Coptic Christian family. The Coptic tradition advocates vegetarianism for 8 to 9 months of the year, where Copts in Egypt fast from dairy and animal products. When the fasting season is over, these semi vegetarians devour huge quantities of meat and dairy. I have always wondered how their hearts could bear the grinding, grilling, and grating of the flesh that belongs to an innocent living and breathing creature.

I could never verbalize the pain that I felt on behalf of the innocent animals that were being exploited day in and day out. This is because most people with a religious background would say: "Since God created these animals and many prophets and saints ate them for years, we too are permitted by God to eat them, and it would be an insult to God to refuse such a gift."

It was not until I started practicing yoga in March 2011, that I learned about the principle of Ahimsa or compassion for all living beings. It was only then that I understood that animals are living, sense pain and pleasure, and have a soul, just like humans; and that we ought to respect them as we do humans.

What breaks my heart is that some people are so out of touch with their feelings that they really believe that animals do not feel pain. Or even worse, they are operating on autopilot to the extent that they don't pause and ask, "Will this animal feel the pain of butchering and other torturous acts?"

In Egypt, it is pretty common to drive down the streets and find butcher shops hanging the flesh of cows and goats in their windows. It is a sickening sight. Even worse, during the Islamic fests, it is customary for each family to slaughter a sheep to offer as a sacrifice to God. And the same families care for dogs and cats. Many of us already feel connected with animals, their warmth, playfulness, compassion, and their ability to communicate and understand; yet how can we be so impersonal with the lives of exploited animals?

I had been vegetarian for 8 years, and as my sensitivity towards animals was refined through yoga and meditation, it became much easier to simply say NO to animal exploitation of any kind.

Billy Leonard, Whangarei, New Zealand

I will always be vegan for ecology. Say what you will about the United Nations—and I know you will—they did release a report or two saying that animal agriculture was the majority cause of greenhouse gas emissions. If you're reading this whilst in a country which has a slaughterhouse economy, this may be news to you. Not that your country has a slaughterhouse economy (you probably knew that already), but that the United Nations released this report and your government took one look at it and then used it to line the birdcages at your capitol building or parliamentary house rather than let you see it.

I will always be vegan for economy. As a professional musket fill, I don't make a lot of money. A musket fill is the feller who goes round all the other fellers on the front lines and refills their muskets with shot. If it was good enough for my great-great-great-great-grandpappy Ezekiel Segal, it's good enough for me. Almost, anyway. I mean, there aren't a lot of musket wars in my neighbourhood anymore. I have to moonlight as a typewriter repairman to make ends meet. Even when Bill Gates, et al, perfect their test-tube meat, and land-and-water issues and animal-suffering concerns are gone by the wayside, I reckon it'll still be cheaper to eat plants than eat the new "Star Trek" diet—especially when ol' Bill realises he forgot to figure in the cost of all those test tubes.

I will always be vegan for laughs. Why would I ever want to give up the kick of telling people I'm vegan and then getting back that they're vegan, too, and, yeah, they eat some fish once in a while?

I will always be vegan for my love life. How else could a short, funny-looking, penniless, middle-aged man have any hope of attracting vegan chicks? Vegan men are that much in demand—for now. Nothing wrong with my social calendar, OK? It's got all the days of the week on it and the days are numbered nice and big so you can read them easily.

Most importantly, I will always be vegan as long as non-human animals have brains and nervous systems—even though my own species seems to lack the brains. Taking the life of an innocent sentient being? Now, that's extreme!

Andreas Thaler, Vienna, Austria

Currently living in Kuala Lumpur, Malaysia

When I was born, 45 years ago, in Austria, it was "logical" that my parents would raise me on a "normal" diet of animal products. I must explain to you that Austria is not just renowned for its music, its beautiful countryside and its rich cultural heritage, but also for its cuisine, which is a mix of the kitchens from the various countries that used to make up the Austrian empire. Italian, Czech, Slovak, Hungarian, Slovenian, Bulgarian, and Romanian dishes have been incorporated into the Austrian kitchen during previous centuries. The downside is that all these dishes, that are delicious for most "normal" people, heavily rely upon animal products.

When I was a small child and found out where "meat" comes from, I was appalled by the fact that animals have to be killed for us to enjoy food, but I also accepted it as "normal". When I was 12 and first heard that there were some people, "vegetarians", who choose not to eat dead animals, I was impressed by their moral fortitude, but equally convinced, that "I could never do that." Around my 20th birthday, I stopped eating meat for some time after having seen a documentary. I found out, to my big surprise, that after a month I had totally lost my craving for meat. For 20 years, I was happily enjoying vegetables, cheese and eggs, and following many traditional vegetarian recipes from Austria's culinary history. I was appalled by people wearing fur coats and very much opposed that—however, I was still using leather, wool and silk, visiting zoos and enjoying other activities like horseback riding, as these were "normal" things to do, even though they relied on animal abuse.

Only five years ago I finally realized that millions of cows and chickens are tortured and killed to produce dairy and eggs. With that knowledge, there was no choice for me but to go vegan, and I made the change quickly. Luckily most recipes can be veganized nowadays, so I do not even need to miss the flavors from my childhood. Once my eyes had been opened to the other various forms of animal (ab)use, I also stopped using animals for clothing, personal hygiene and entertainment by finding suitable alternatives.

Will I always live vegan? Yes. To be very honest, I cannot think of anything else that would be acceptable to me for the rest of my life. Having once had my eyes opened to the horrors of animal products, I simply cannot "choose" to start participating in this circle of death again.

Shlomi Hillel, Haifa, Israel

Between Good and Evil

Who does not occasionally do bad things?

We all hurt our friends at times, gossip, even lie. We reassure ourselves that next time we will be better, kinder, more decent, and considerate. And even in childhood we were taught to respect others and not exploit their weaknesses.

But how would you react if you were told that you were an unwitting accomplice in a cruel institution of merciless torture and mass killings?

In 2010 it dawned on me that I had been participating in such an institution—the institution of animal exploitation. Humans exploit other animals for food, clothing, scientific research, and entertainment. We kill more animals for food in five days than all humans killed in wars and genocides in recorded human history.

Each and every one of these animals is a living, sentient being; an individual. In their short wretched life, each one of them is treated in ways that would be considered torture if inflicted on a human. Their miserable life is taken so that we can enjoy, for a few fleeting minutes, their flesh, or the milk and eggs stolen while they were still alive. Each one of them is, after all, merely an economic unit, a currency.

We all agree that it is wrong to harm animals unnecessarily. But we do not have to consume meat, dairy, or eggs. In fact, animal products can be detrimental to our health. Pleasure, habit, or convenience cannot justify inflicting unnecessary suffering and death, either. We have no justification for the continued exploitation of animals.

Two insights had eluded me for many years before I became vegan. The first is that it is possible to be vegan and healthy, and the second is that animals have moral significance. Today, it is hard for me to believe that I was comfortable living with silly excuses while I was funding a cruel industry. Every single day I regret the meat and cheese that I put in my mouth before becoming vegan.

I will never again in my life contribute to the exploitation of animals—I will always be vegan. I will continue to object to this abominable institutionalized exploitation until my last breath.

Rae Sikora, New Mexico, USA

I will always be vegan because veganism is not a diet. For me, being vegan is about making choices that align with my most loving values. I love all animals, I love the beautiful natural world around us, I love caring for my own health, and I care about all people. The best way I can show that LOVE is to practice veganism every day, every moment. Sometimes I wish there was another word for VEGAN because too many people think it is a fad or a diet. I want a word that expresses how it makes me feel like I am a walking heart and that I can make my choices from that most loving place. I will always be vegan because I do not need to eat animal products or wear them, I do not need to use any products tested on other species, and I can easily entertain myself without supporting industries that imprison animals and display them or make them do tricks. When I make these choices I feel GREAT physically and emotionally and spiritually. My life is joyful, healthy and rich, and I am surrounded by a compassionate community. I am almost 60 years old and I feel like I am still in my twenties… Thank you healthy vegan choices!

Alfredo Kuba, California, USA

I am vegan because no one should have to suffer or die for me or anyone else to exist. I simply could not live with myself knowing that I am the cause of a fellow living, feeling, breathing being's suffering and death; the thought of it revolts me. I am a vegan because of them, not because of me. Because their lives matter.

I am vegan because the alternative is a social evil just like slavery or the holocaust, but much much worse—billions of times worse—because of the number of animals tortured and killed. It must be abolished. I am a vegan because I do not want to be a part of "the taking of life" for the sake of mine. I am a vegan because I would rather die before taking the life of another more helpless and innocent being than I, who deserves to live. We are such a self-righteous species, so arrogant and so evil, and so above all of nature and life. We so easily and systematically mass murder billions of innocent beings. We devour them, wear them, cut them up in laboratories, and enslave and exploit them for amusement and fun.

I choose a different path, the vegan path. That is why I am vegan.

Drawing 'I know what you're going to go through' by Jo Frederiks - www.jofrederiks.com

Helen Liakopoulos, **Montreal, Canada**

My vegan lifestyle is in my soul... One way to explain my reason for being vegan is by telling the story of the cow. This is an analogy that I feel represents my reasons.

A person once asked me about a picture of a black and white image. He asked me, what do I see? When I initially looked, all I saw was lots of black spots. In my eyes, it was a picture of a black and white image. I could not see anything else. The person said to me to look deeper. I looked again and tried to focus on the image. They encouraged me to look again. It may have taken me a while, but I finally saw the cow. I feel that I saw the cow only because they inspired me to keep looking and to stay focused. Had I been left alone to analyze the photo, I am not sure I would have seen the cow.

I will always be a vegan because once you have seen the truth, just like the "cow" image, it's impossible to not see the reality of animal cruelty. As a vegan I feel the same way. The "cow" represents animal suffering, and once I had a shift in consciousness and saw that animals suffer needlessly it was hard for me to ever go back. I see the injustice when the animals suffer, when we take their babies away. I see the softness of nature when a baby animal is searching for his/her parent; they cuddle, kiss, play and enjoy each other's company just as humans do. When a baby animal learns to walk it looks the same way human babies do. It must be the way baby animal teeth grow in, just as adorable as human babies' teeth; they have the same innocent look.

Honestly, they all ask why I am a vegan—it is very simple, I've seen the "cow". I don't see a black and white image anymore. I feel I have a responsibility to be a role model. I want to show the world that we are capable of living a cruelty-free lifestyle. We do not need to hurt animals for any purpose. This is why my soul will always be vegan. My wish is that one day all of humanity will see the "cow".

Neil Kaplan, Florida, USA

About 25 years ago I was trying to change the direction of my life by taking the Lifespring self-improvement course. How could I have foreseen just how this goal was going to manifest itself? A woman who was also attending the seminar introduced me to the idea of being vegetarian for ethical reasons. From there, through a number of experiences and insights over several years, I became vegetarian, and eventually vegan.

The challenge with veganism isn't the diet…following a healthy, plant-based diet has been easy for me. The difficult part is that as we learn more about the insane cruelty inflicted on other animals by humans, it overwhelms our consciousness. We begin to feel the pain of every animal killed on a factory farm, shot by a hunter, or subjected to painful product testing. We become aware of the suffering of every fish caught on a line or in a net, every bull tortured by a matador, every cat and dog put down because there just aren't homes for them, every mother cow having her newborn calf stolen away, and so many more horrors…we feel it all personally. We know that every one of these creatures had a life, had feelings, had a sense of self. We know that as that fish was struggling for breath, as the pig was waiting to have his throat slit, as that rabbit was having caustic chemicals put in her eyes…they all were desperate for rescue, for relief, and wondering "why?"

Being vegan isn't only about food; it's about kindness and compassion. As vegans, we cannot go back to being a part of a system that inflicts deliberate pain and death on billions of sentient animals every year. Rather, it falls upon us to do everything we can to change it, to raise human consciousness, to strive for a day when every person will understand what we have already come to recognize. We envision a day when the cages will be open, when non-human animals will be valued for the individuals they are, and not only for whatever value they might have as a "product" for human consumption. I am vegan, and will be for life.

Max Stewart, Tucson, Arizona, USA

There are millions of animals in the world, thousands of varieties, each creature home to an infinite number of unique characteristics. By exploiting animals for human gain, we affect every animal's existence through a startling chain of events; forests are brutally mutilated for farmland, excessive agriculture causes droughts, and animal breeding is manipulated to achieve human goals for production for clothing, food, and entertainment when superior choices are easily available. Every animal that is used in farming, entertainment, and clothing was a potential companion, best friend, or interesting creature to observe. To lose the opportunity to see the mannerisms and interactions of any animal is to lose a whole culture, bound and processed into the grey monotone of exploitation. The twisting of an animal's nature in zoos and circuses simply distorts the beauty of their natural ways. It is absolutely illogical to see prisons, torture, and death sentences as disgusting and inhumane, while the way animals are treated in human industry is seen as completely acceptable.

Among the most deplorable aspects of the exploitation of animals is the utter inefficiency of animal industry. Humans are not obligate carnivores, nor do we need animal-based clothing, therefore the massive amounts of water used in the dairy and leather industries (that causes droughts), and the swathes of farmland used just to grow food for domesticated animals, is absurd. A simple biological fact is that, as animals eat animals that eat plants, energy is being lost in the process, so alternative resources are more efficient. If humans lived vegan and did not devote so much energy to dominating animals, less land would be wasted, more food and clothing would be produced more cheaply, and animal abuse would be significantly reduced. Veganism is the superior economic choice.

Notably, the typical human's deepest fear is of discovering a superior, unconquerable animal; we fear someone more powerful than us, someone who could eat, enslave, or use us without consent. Most extra-terrestrial or paranormal stories are based in this fear of the omniscient. We do not seem to realize that our deepest fears are the reality that animals live, on a daily basis. I will always be vegan because it is fundamentally hypocritical to fear the destruction of our human civilization, when those who exploit animals are doing the same to every other living being; veganism is the most sensible option.

Gina Seraichyk, Rhode Island, USA

I imagine there is a planet that looks very much like Earth. It is inhabited by creatures that are exactly like human beings, except that they are far more gentle, intelligent and civilized than most of us. They are the only species of living creature on their planet. In their quest for greater knowledge they travel to Earth to observe us. They are amazed to see how similar our planet is to theirs, and surprised to see the humans who look just like them.

Within the first few hours of their visit they discover the non-human creatures. They are awestruck by the beauty and diversity of the various creatures. The human beings living here are extraordinarily lucky! These non-human creatures fly, swim and hop. Some are brilliantly colorful, some have bodies that are masterpieces of engineering design, some make unique and lovely noises, and some are absurdly adorable. Whoever created these creatures was surely an artistic and comedic genius! This place must be the realization of a god's fantasy.

Within days, they come to some peculiar realizations. The humans here eat the creatures?! They also steal some of them to keep as companions against their will, force them to perform various difficult tasks, use their live bodies for scientific experiments, strip them of their skin, feathers and fur, and shoot at them, among countless other strange atrocities. A few of the more fortunate animals have somehow eluded the humans. A few others seem happy under human care. However, for the most part, the humans appear to have little or no regard at all for these beautiful earthlings that are different from them. This place is not paradise, but some sort of cruel nightmare. The aliens are so utterly perplexed by this situation that they leave in despair and confusion. They cannot imagine an explanation for the frightful situation on planet Earth.

What separates us from the animals? The animals are not motivated by greed. Of all the offensive and hurtful words: the "N" word, the "R" word... For me the most horrible is the "L" word: livestock. What could be more blatantly evil than breeding living beings for the purpose of using them like things?

I am vegan because I'd like to believe that I have more in common with the non-human animals than I do with human beings. I will always be vegan because the animals are my family.

Chrissy Halliday, Sydney, Australia

If I could reduce my experience of veganism to a single word, then I would say it has been "illuminating". From the moment I made the change, it was as if a bright light had been switched on, casting light across previously darkened places; most of which were buried deep in my mind. I saw who I was more clearly and I couldn't hide behind myths and false logic anymore. I couldn't ignore the fact that my decisions had catastrophic results for non-human persons. Their blood was on my hands and I felt guilty and ashamed for being complicit.

Being vegan liberated me and has brought the world into a much clearer focus than it had been previously. While I don't discount the various benefits to personal and environmental health and wellbeing, such concerns are not my motivation for being vegan. For me, being vegan is a social justice issue. It embodies, in both thought and deed, the understanding that it is morally wrong to enslave sentient beings for human benefit. It is about recognising that non-human persons have the same right to life that we claim for ourselves.

The concept of veganism is an absolute: a person either rejects slavery or supports it. There is no middle ground. Being vegan has taught me there is no absolution to be found in seeking a right way to do wrong things. And for me, using animals for my own personal gain is morally unjustifiable. My desire to eliminate the suffering of non-human persons is strong, and prohibits me from ever being tempted to participate in anything that causes harm. But it is also my recognition of their rights that equips me with the tools necessary to advocate on their behalf.

Being vegan is not a "diet", nor should it ever be confused with one. It is the philosophical foundation on which all my decisions are based. The possibility of not being vegan doesn't exist for me. To do so would be to abandon my values, and I can't live my life in conflict with what I know to be true and right. I can't undo my previous wrongs. But every day, for the rest of my life, I will seek to atone for past sins. I will always be vegan because there isn't a single justifiable reason for me not to be.

Isabel Gonzalez Garcia, Lisbon, Portugal

Two years ago here in Portugal, I was looking for images on the internet to use in a protest against using animal fur. I found one picture showing a terrified baby fox in a cage with the message "If you know what is going to happen to him, how could you allow it?"

Correct questions have the power to shake our heads upside down, and after those questions usually come many more, like "How can I consider myself an animal lover if I eat animals?" or "Do I really know what all these caged animals have to go through waiting for death?" Many documentaries later, and after many tears and nights spent looking for information, the answers did not feel like a wall falling over, but like recovering a part of myself that was silenced and ignored for decades.

I thought I knew the meaning of the words "respect", "justice", and "empathy", but in that moment it was clear to me that I did not understand the deeper significance of them. From a very early age, we have to accept as correct the premise that dogs are friends and calves are food; that some lives are more important than others, and that animals are here to serve our purposes. But these premises are not correct. We grow up thinking we have the right to take from animals everything we want (their lives, their babies, their food, their homes …), but this is not true, we don't have that right; it is just that simple.

Now, I not only know exactly what happens to baby foxes in fur farms, but to all the animals in other farms, aquariums, and all sort of cages waiting for their turn to die; murdered for no reason other than greed. I see clearly that I don't want to be part of it. I want to fight against this horror. To me, veganism means the first and minimum step we have to take to stop the injustice and abuse of animals. The first step is to respect their lives. Vegan activism is the only way to avoid the unjustified oppression, exploitation and suffering humans cause to animals. I will always do as much as I can to get rid of all the cages for animals, and I will certainly always be vegan.

Balabhadra Bruce Costain, USA

Canadian living in Nashville, Tennessee

I grew up in a non-veg family with hunting and fishing as part of our lifestyle. Many of my extended family were farmers. Non-veg was my diet for approximately 35 years. In college I was introduced to a meditation program and undertook the daily practice. I mention this because I think (in retrospect) meditation activated the change of consciousness that resulted in later adopting a vegetarian, and short time later, vegan diet.

While in college I attended a lecture on Jainism, which was my introduction to vegetarianism, Ahimsa/non-harming, and reverence for all life. Vegetarianism was intriguing and, with the help of the Seventh Day Adventists, this diet was adopted. A trip to India and further exposure to Hindu-Jain cultures of Ahimsa practice motivated me to attend grad school, which resulted in my Ph.D. entitled: *An Ethic of Reverence for All Life as the Basis for Human Development*. The thesis argues that non-harming and compassion toward all living beings are characteristics of one's Soul. As the Soul is "purified" veganism will be the natural disposition. And conversely, veganism is a necessary disposition for the Soul to reach its full potential.

My interest and commitment to veganism is basically selfish. I am selfish for the joy that vegan living brings:

- Joy that I am no longer part of the "horror" involved in the production of so-called "meat". I have been to the slaughterhouses and witnessed the horror that occurs. My self-righteousness is softened by the fact that in my earlier life I participated in the killing of chickens, pigs, rabbits, groundhogs, etc. These memories still cause me to cringe.

- Joy that occurs with the vegan/Ahimsa "live and let live" lifestyle. It is joyful, fun in fact, to avoid exploiting other creatures big and small.

- Joy (and freedom) that the fear of diet related health problems are eliminated. As proof, I am 70 years old, have been vegan for 32 years to date, and still have great health and vitality.

- Joy that I (along with a larger community of other vegan/vegetarians) am trying to minimize the adverse effect of my existence on the environment of our deteriorating planet.

For me, veganism is an aspect of Ahimsa consciousness which involves Awe and Reverence for the mystery of existence of which all living beings are a part; and a natural disposition to "do no harm" in all aspects of Life.

Douglas R. Geovanini, Brazil

Vegan activist for animal rights

Once you wake up to the harsh reality imposed on animals, to the impact of speciesism on their lives, you simply reject every kind of animal use and do not want to contribute in any way.

Initially I understood the violence that they face through text, pictures and videos. Nowadays I realize that the problem is beyond the cruelty, and that it is wrong to use them as property per se, regardless of the treatment they receive. They are not objects, they are not property.

I also understand that the view of society needs to change. A speciesist view is one that feeds the idea that we can exploit them for not being humans. The prejudice against species—speciesism—is the root of all animal exploitation.

Here is a little about the trajectory of my perception since I became vegan. I believe that both considerations below are good examples that veganism, consciously practiced, based on animal rights, is not a style, a religion, or a particular opinion, and shows precisely that it is something urgent, primordial and a consolidated attitude I will have until the end of my life.

NEED - Simply, we human beings do not need to use animals for food, clothing, entertainment or any other anthropocentric purpose. Any "need" claimed is just pleasure, amusement, convenience and culture; ethically unjustifiable and perfectly condemnable from the broadest point of view that analyzes every sentient being involved. If it is not a human need and we have the possibility to choose, we should put "animal rights" in practice (veganism).

DUTIES - More than a right choice or practice, veganism is a human obligation, because when we talk about veganism we talk about respect for animals, and respect is mandatory. Let's take our neighbors as examples. Assuming that we don't know them well, thus we don't have enough closeness to like them. However, we have the obligation to respect them. The same is true with animals. There are people that live away from a rural reality and don't know or love some animals. Indeed, they don't really need to know or love them, but similar to their neighbors, they have the obligation of respect!

This is veganism; it is the least we humans can do to see and treat animals as someone and not something. For these concrete facts I will always be vegan!

Dr. Sylvia Irawati, M. Gizi, Indonesia

Love and compassion—I believe they are two things that keep this universe surviving, and being vegan is a part of it.

Knowing about veganism and being a vegan myself—where veganism is uncommon in my country except for religious reasons—is such a great blessing the universe gave me. Since I became vegan two years ago, it seems that I've been awakened from a long sleep and reconnected with the universe. I see the world in a different way; that I am just a small part of it and that all living beings are connected.

Being vegan taught me to live in peace with my inner being and with every living creature around me. I see life in everything—in trees, in flowers, in pets, in farm animals, even in insects—and there is no right to destroy it. Apart from the health benefit from being vegan, it brings me more energy to be positive in mind and to share that positivity with people around me. My friends and family realize that somehow I became more calm and peaceful after being a vegan.

Since being vegan changed me to a better person and gives me a more peaceful and meaningful life, I will never trade it for anything. Being vegan is not a choice, it is the only right way to live, and that's the reason I will always be vegan.

Photo provided by Karrel Christopher - www.karrelchristopher.com

Eriyah Flynn, Columbus, Ohio, USA

If I ever wanted to be worthy of living, it was necessary to be a person who lived with integrity, courage, honor and in consistency with my values, for truth, liberty, justice, respect, dignity, equality, empathy, kindness, compassion and peace for all earthlings. I will never be able to undo what I have unconsciously and unquestioningly participated in for far too long as I was developing in the non-vegan, discriminative, deceptive, disconnected programming culture I inherited.

Though I am viscerally saddened in discovering the magnitude of unnecessary, horrific and violent reality that is at every foundation of humanity's present course of soul killing, animal killing, world killing, self-fulfilling, self-destructing, what I can do now is make a stand to change the course of that world for the direction that I would see us have. I have never felt more alive, driven or committed to a life of purpose and passion as I have since I unplugged from the marketing matrix and awakened from the trance of currently dominant American culture of dysfunctional and misdirected priorities obsessed with blind consumerism, materialism, entertainment, sports, celebrity culture, and a "what's in it for me" mentality.

It is a powerful thing to know I am not alone on this mission; that there are in fact millions of vegans moving this world in the most awesomely epic odyssey for human consciousness and advancement towards peace ever undertaken in our history. It is a beautiful thing to know that no matter one's family history, religion, gender, age, sexual orientation, ability, career, etc., we can decide to live vegan.

Photo provided by Karrel Christopher - www.karrelchristopher.com

100

Lisa Bennett, Maidenhead, England

Becoming vegan has been one of the biggest defining points of my life. We all search for them—these defining moments—through our relationships with others, through religion or spirituality, through enduring physical challenges to our bodies and in our environment. Every one of us is on a different path, but I think most of us want the same thing: to leave this world knowing that we lived a full life, and that we have grown into a better person during our time here. I've experienced two different religions and my fair share of relationships so far in my life, including motherhood. I have spent the first half of my life in one country and the second half in another. I have done quite a bit of travelling. I've got some life experience in my 54 years. As a result, I feel that every step of the journey has helped me discover my truest self in veganism.

Even as a vegetarian for 17 years, I knew deep down that I could do more, and that feeling stayed with me until I finally chose veganism seven years ago. Veganism offers a spiritual fulfilment that transcends any experience of oneness with the Divine that religion could offer. It is true compassion, true selflessness and brings an incomparable feeling of wholeness to know that I am choosing not to engage in violence against any sentient creature. I can look any animal (including human) straight in the eye and feel a connection to that being that I never felt before I was vegan. It's almost indescribable, but it is a fullness of heart that other vegans will understand and recognise. It's not "praying" for a better future. It is BEING a better future; right now. I get to be the best possible example of humanity in THIS life.

The rewards of veganism go deeper. I have discovered that my food choices have not diminished, but expanded. I am trying new things, I have learned to cook and love it! I now spend my Sundays volunteering at an animal shelter, and it is the best job I have ever had, because the feeling it gives me is better than money. Committing to veganism has made me FREE to explore life unfettered, causing the least harm possible to our planet. Veganism is a gift that I would never trade. It's the secret to a happy life.

Oorvashi Panchoo, Republic of Mauritius

I am a vegan for life because, above all reasons, my heart is in it. Having been vegan for quite some time now, there's no turning back. There are no obvious excuses for wanting someone to die unnecessarily to become a meal. A video showing how the cows are treated on dairy farms and how their babies are torn away from them proved me guilty in consuming dairy products.

Life had always seemed fair to me since I entered this world. Being born into a vegetarian family, I was used to dairy products, honey, wearing and using animal skins. It just never occurred to me that I was unintentionally participating in the misery of thousands of farmed animals, until I came across this video of a dairy farm. Was life indeed fair to everyone?

Searching for non-dairy alternatives led me to veganism. I learnt more about the suffering and misery our animal brothers and sisters face due to the meat, dairy, egg and fur industries. Never had I thought of such unimaginable torture inflicted on these innocent beings. I became vegan for the animals, and now I do my best to help other people open their eyes and hearts to their pain—because I agree that many participate in their suffering unknowingly. No taste in the world can be worth someone's life, and the couldn't-live-without cheese is now a piece of blood to me.

I will always remain vegan, because I know that the animals have done nothing for mankind to inflict such pain onto them. I will remain vegan to help our mother, the Planet Earth, to replenish and to blossom in beauty. I will always be vegan, because I know that by taking this one step, thousands of people may be saved from starvation. It was only after becoming vegan that I realised how beautiful the word "vegan" is, and how beautiful the world would be, if everyone was vegan.

Photo by El Hogar ProVegan animal sanctuary, Spain - www.elhogarprovegan.org

Elizabeth Wolf, Newcastle, Australia

I will always be vegan because it is part of who I am. I have spent more of my life living, breathing and eating as a vegan, and I am so very grateful to all the people I met and articles that I read in the late 1980s that changed my way of thinking and led me to veganism. Once I learnt about the inherent cruelties of the meat, dairy, egg, fish, honey, silk, leather, wool, fur, etc. industries, I could no longer eat, drink, wear any of these products.

I will always be vegan because I raised two babies to adults who are life vegans; Jarius (19) and Khadi (23). I have a very deep connection to them. I nourished them via breast feeding till they self-weaned, and made them strong in heart, hands and health. I have led my children along the path of compassion, animal liberation, Ahimsa, vegan wholefoods, equality and environmental awareness within in a world of carnage, destruction, war, slaughterhouses, speciesism and racism. I've shown them through my lifestyle and parenting with my husband Stephen (also a long-time vegan) that they are part of a positive, life affirming way of life.

And that is why I will always be vegan.

Photo by C-A-L-F Sanctuary, United Kingdom

103

Cameron Johnston, Ontario, Canada

The question "Why will I always be vegan?" is the same as asking "What is a human being?" or "What is human nature?" To ask this is to carefully consider what I can hope for, and what I should do.

The answer is based on the entire history of humanity and this planet, and points to our place in life and the place of each of Earth's creatures in the whole of existence.

The answer is that I will always be vegan because of what we have learned from human history. We have learned that we are ethical beings, driven by moral concerns about the consequences of what we think and do, and motivated by how this relates to all others. We have learned that those consequences are ultimate, in the sense that they create the conditions of existence and our place within it. We know that the existence that we must realize is community and harmony with all life.

My place as a human being is to take care of all of this beautiful life and to stand in awe and wonder. A person who does this is called "vegan" but in reality this is the core of what we are.

Photo by C-A-L-F Sanctuary, United Kingdom

Faris Said Nassoro, Kenya, Africa

Allow me to introduce myself, I am Faris Said Nassoro; I am a man living in Mombasa Kenya, in Africa. My English is not that good so you will excuse me for any misunderstandings.

I choose to be a vegan because when I was a small boy I had a rabbit as a pet; I loved her, was proud of her, and boasted to my friends about her. I took good care of her, cleaning her place of sleeping, bringing food from our small farm. In fact she was part of me and the closest friend of that time. One day when I came back from school, I didn't find my rabbit friend; I ran everywhere looking for her, she was nowhere to be seen. I cried asking my mum where my rabbit was. She first asked me to cool down, then she explained to me that while I was at school my aunt (dad's sister) came to visit us. She didn't have money to entertain her, therefore she decided to slaughter my rabbit and fry it for my aunt. I was helpless, couldn't do anything, went on crying for two days, mourning and thinking of my lovely and close friend who was turned to food just to entertain an unexpected guest. I swore on that day not to eat any kind of meat or fish, and I have stuck to my oath ever since.

I am now proud to be a vegan. There are a lot of benefits of eating vegetables rather than eating meat or fish. In vegetables we find a lot of vitamins, minerals and medicinal attributes, and all are in favour of our health. I argue all humans should try, even for one month, to be vegetarian and experience what comes of their health. You will find only one in a million true vegetarian suffering from cancer, diabetes or even abnormalities of blood pressure. That's goodness for being a vegan.

We have to protect animals, they have a right to exist and they have a purpose to be here among us. It hurts a lot to see poachers here in Africa and especially here in Kenya shooting and killing elephants and rhino only for their tusks and horns. Let us unite from every corner of our planet and stand together in one voice, let us choose veganism as our way of life. Being vegan, our planet is going to be a peaceful and harmonious one. Vegan is the right choice.

Sæunn Ingibjörg, Marinósdóttir, Iceland

I will always be vegan. Veganism is the core of my being. It represents everything I believe to be true and right. Following the vegan path is to me a lifelong commitment that constantly brings me to new levels of compassion and tranquillity. It started with my opposition to the consumption of animal flesh, evolved into rejecting any animal based foods, then led me to understand the problems of wearing clothes made out of animal materials, and now I simply refuse any violence or exploitation of animals or people.

Today, my veganism has expanded into not wanting to cause harm to any species or form of life and it has abolished my desire for unnecessary things of any kind. I have gained a deeper understanding of life and my awe of non-human animals can on occasions bring me to tears. Veganism has taught me respect, gratitude and minimalism. It is an emotionally complex state that has brought me tremendous serenity and passion at the same time, while causing extreme pain and sorrow by forcing me to face the horror and violence our species practices every second of every day. The sum of my experiences gives me the absolute affirmation of my continued vegan journey and the importance of my stance. I reject the idea that consuming or exploiting animals in any way is a choice for us to make. Nobody has given me or other humans the power of manipulating, torturing or killing non-human persons for our own gain or to temporarily satisfy our greed. We simply have no right, and to those who insist that nobody has proven that animals are sentient, I respond: it has not been proven that they are not.

Some people accuse vegans of extremism, as if there could ever be too much peace and love in the world. Even if it's possible to be excessively peaceful and non-violent, I'm happy to be an ambassador of a movement that gives all life the benefit of any doubt that may still be present. The reason why I will always be vegan is that I have no reason not to be. It's extremely easy, it can do no harm and it minimizes the suffering my existence could cause in this world. Veganism is my philosophical and political statement. I believe it to be the answer to many of our world's problems and I simply could not comprehend any regression.

С уважением, **Konshina Kseniya, Russia**

Here in Russia we have a lot of vegans. We have a vegan power-lifting team and a lot of vegan websites, and even an animal rights center. Every day we fight for animal rights, and today we have laws to punish cruelty to animals.

As for me, I have been vegan since 2008 and now I am 24 years old. I became a vegan because of my ethical views. Because of what is inside of me. I don't know why I decided to be vegan at first, but I do know I have no reasons to eat meat and wear fur or leather, even living in Russia. I have no need to do it. In winter, we have low temperatures near -25 or -30C but I wear coats without fur or bird's fuzz, and it is warm enough for me. For me, a life is a sacred gift from an invisible power and I know that I have no right to kill somebody without any ponderable reasons. And of course I know how "livestock" negatively impacts the Earth. I love my planet and I love animals, and I hope people will understand how important it is to care about them.

Angela McAninly, **Australia**

I don't need 400 words to explain why I will always be vegan. For me it boils down to the simplest of reasons: I CAN be vegan, therefore I am. I am a thinking person. I have choices. I have opened my heart to the plight of non-human animals being bred and raised for purposes that are not their own. I recognise that being vegan is a powerful force to combat climate change. I have empathy for the Third-World child who starves while we in the affluent West gorge ourselves on food that is not only unnecessary, but which is making us sick. I do not need meat, dairy, or eggs. I do not need leather, silk or wool. And I never have needed them. Waking up to that fact was like seeing the sun rise to illuminate a beautiful future of compassion, nonviolence and love. I CAN be vegan...so MY question would be: "Why wouldn't I?"

Samuel Gerard, California, USA

Why I will ALWAYS be vegan…

Because I didn't choose to be a human…I just happen to be one…

Because I appreciate being treated with compassion, empathy, kindness and respect…

Because I treat EVERY sentient being as I want to be treated…

Because I'd die before taking the life of an innocent peaceful sentient being.

Anastasia Lipapis, ACT, Australia

Always vegan…for all of the years I wasn't…for all of the suffering I've witnessed in photos and footage that has turned my stomach.

Always vegan…for the lives of so many; for the suffering aplenty…for the madness on this planet continues.

Always vegan…for the millions of those who are voiceless…for the millions with beauty that's stolen…for all the pain that goes unaccounted.

Always vegan…for now my eyes are opened…they always see what's often unspoken.

Always vegan…always!

Michael Bowman, New Hampshire, USA

To ask why I will always be vegan is like asking why I will always not be racist. Why will I always be against sexism? Why will I always be against discrimination? Injustice is injustice. We can forgive those who have been racist or sexist in the distant past, but that doesn't mean we're not critical of them. Even with the social standards of the time, we still talk about how heartless it was and how atrocious they were. I want to be among those who can say "I didn't stand for it. I wasn't impassive to evil." There is an infamous poem about WW2 by Martin Niemöller which finitely defines the dangers of indifference:

"First they came for the Socialists, and I did not speak out –
Because I was not a Socialist.
Then they came for the Trade Unionists, and I did not speak out –
Because I was not a Trade Unionist.
Then they came for the Jews, and I did not speak out –
Because I was not a Jew.
Then they came for me – and there was no one left to speak for me."

However, in this case, indifference is even more dangerous because the Socialists had a voice, and the Trade Unionists and the Jews had voices which they could use to speak up. The animals have only their distinguished cries of sorrow, which translate both universally and into no language we speak at all.

Happy meat isn't happy. It's dead. I can't say I've met many optimistic dead people. Exploitation is exploitation. Abuse is abuse. Until the day comes when we no longer accept such exploitation, we must not only be vegan, but persuade others to be vegan. To say it's a choice to be vegan is forgetting a certain individual: the animal. It's not just compassion. It's justice. I won't just be vegan. I will be an animal rights activist. I will be the voice for the animals.

Vicki Xirakia, Volos, Greece

I always loved animals. Ever since a little child, I was fascinated by their complexity and felt compassion towards them. The first seeds of veganism were planted in my heart when I saw my grandfather slaughtering a baby goat. Just the previous afternoon I was hugging and playing with the goat; whose name was Billy. I will never forget his scream as the knife cut his throat. I was shocked at how easily a life had been taken just for the mere pleasure of a couple of meals. I could never look at meat in the same way. To me, it always looked like a corpse, like the remains of a living, breathing, conscious being. Once the connection is made, between what (or who) we see on our plates and where it comes from, the wall separating butcher shop from slaughterhouse is shattered forever and the truth cannot be unseen. I refuse to feast on death. I chose life and love.

It became clear to me that non-human animals exist for their own purposes, they are not here for us to exploit for profit. They are sentient beings who feel pain, pleasure, fear, happiness. They deserve to be free. Their place is not in the factory farm, not in the laboratory, not in the zoo, not in the circus. Today, I am a mom and I hope to inspire my son to work towards building a better planet for all of us; humans and non-humans. He has never tasted flesh, dairy, eggs, or honey. He has never worn animal skins or wool, and he has never been to the zoo or circus. He is pure and loving and truly compassionate towards all beings, no matter how small. For him, a cow is a sheep is a dog. All equal, all worthy. I am teaching him to listen to his heart, to love unconditionally the beauty around him, to be brave and stand up for justice, and to be the voice for the voiceless. And maybe one day, the world will be a better place for all of us.

Photo by El Hogar ProVegan animal sanctuary, Spain - www.elhogarprovegan.org   110

Véronique Perrot, France

Going Home

When you get personal with certain beings, you automatically see their personality. But when it comes to all the others that are invisible to you, they simply don't matter. What we do three times a day is ignore the very beings who are right there on our plates and dismiss them as just food—the same way we ignore the ones in the wild, zoos, and circuses as just strangers or things to play with. We don't know who they were, what they felt, how they died, and how they suffered to satisfy just a few minutes of selfish pleasure.

But one day, I came back home to my heart; to my innate compassion. I went vegan. I was born one, it had simply been repressed by my parents, society, governments, religions, and the media, assisted by the ability of humans to deny their inner truths and willingness to avoid what is uncomfortable. I had only forgotten who I truly was.

As a child growing up in France, I ate the steak and cheese my mother gave me. It was just that: meat and cheese. It had no other name. I went to see animals in circuses, they were amusing. That is all I was thinking about. No one told me they all once had real lives as breathing, feeling beings or that I helped steal milk from a grieving mother who wanted to give it to her baby. Schools don't teach us to be good people towards all beings, they teach us to be unquestioning robots who follow society's orders.

It is hard at times to be vegan in France. Even the word "vegan" is still alien to most people. But I would rather lose friends, family, and "traditions", than lose my ethics. Whether people mock me or embrace me (and the latter is more often what happens), this is something that is above me. I am defined by my mission to eliminate the suffering of other animals whoever they are and help those who want to join a new vegan world.

Without vegans to point out what is wrong with our world, we will all perish. The truth is that the Earth and other animals can live without us, but we can't survive without them. To be vegan is to eliminate this false separation between us and all the beings who share this beautiful planet with us, and to create peace.

Dra. Ana María Aboglio, Argentina

The Other Vision

Whenever we shake up our lives with a decision, we are always moved to a place from which we cannot revert back to our former selves. Sometimes, of course, we may end up somewhere we regret and so go back. But this is not possible when an entirely new way of seeing makes an impact on us and becomes an integral part of who we are.

Emerging from this new vision comes a critical examination of the current situation endured by other animals. Upon empathizing with these other consciousnesses, all sentient as humans, each oppressed individual interpellates, foreign to the idea of the social construct labeled "species". With these transformative encounters with animals who take us into the world of the other, it is unnecessary to understand exactly "what it feels like to be a bat".

We know that all sentient beings have interests in making the most of their lives and in continuing to live, and that there is no reason whatsoever to deny them the opportunity to fulfil those interests. From that, intention and desire are merged in the pursuit of not causing harm to them.

The other vision that I am proposing in order to traverse this world, moving away from a position of arrogance, rejecting the obstinate tendency to dominate or control, will allow the space for veganism to become situated as the immutable baseline of the principle of respect.

This is because it is a way of seeing which is capable of revealing what is hidden by anthropocentrism, dissolving the moral opacities that cloud the reality of what is driving the arbitrary discrimination borne by non-human animals. In addition, this other vision signifies a recognition that there are others observing the world through their own senses.

I propose that we embrace these perspectives, restoring to other animals the dignity they deserve, and of which we have deprived them. From there, I will always advocate veganism as being a practice of justice and equality.

Taylor Wyers, **Barrie, Ontario, Canada**

I will always be vegan because I know that humans are not superior to animals, and that we are all equals—every one of us. I refuse to sit back idly as animals are tortured for our own sick pleasure and entertainment. We do not need meat or animal products to survive, and we especially do not need to torture these innocent beings. I am not vegan simply because I do not agree with the meat industry; I am also vegan because I don't agree with how dairy cows are treated, or how animals are confined to tiny tanks and cages just so that we can spend a day watching them. I don't agree with the way animals are forced to suffer just so that we can have a nice smelling perfume or a perfect lipstick. I do not agree with using animals for anything.

I will always be vegan because I want to prove to the world that we can live alongside animals, peacefully, without using them as resources or entertainment. We believe that we need to use animals for food, but vegans everywhere prove that statement is not true. Animals deserve love and compassion, and they deserve to live freely without being confined to small, disgusting spaces. They deserve to live without having their offspring ripped away from them, and without having to experience mass amounts of suffering just to please us. I cannot stand the thought of eating something that feels, and that felt an awful lot of pain and suffering just for me to enjoy a meal. Animals have rights. They deserve the same freedom as we do. That is why I will always be vegan.

Photo provided by Karrel Christopher - www.karrelchristopher.com

Gro Ottesen, Stavanger, Norway

I am a vegan for life because I went vegan for my love for all animals. I am also an animal rights activist, which I see as my obligation.

I was vegetarian for 18 years. I did not know the ugly truth about the dairy industry. I watched a brilliant speech online, and after about 15 minutes the speaker started to talk about how calves were taken from their mothers. I cried and cried and went vegan right there. I got my children to watch it as well, and the same happened with them. Our entire family are vegans and the youngest one is 11 months old.

We do different kinds of activism. My son rescued a horse that was on the way to the slaughterhouse. He is a happy horse today. Running free with his herd. No horseback riding as we are totally against all use of animals.

We don't look at animal products as food; neither do my grandchildren. We are the biggest vegan family in Norway, and I can say that after such an awakening it is impossible to even think of not being vegan for the rest of our lives.

Photo provided by Karrel Christopher - www.karrelchristopher.com

Vanda Kadas, Hungary/California, USA

I grew up in Hungary, a small country with lots of old traditions and history. One of the most popular traditions of my hometown, "Sausage Town", was to raise pigs for slaughter. My grandparents also had a small homestead which was seemingly like a "pig spa". While our "domestic animals" were "treated humanely" and with "compassion", we decided the moment their lives ended: the moment we, in cold-blood, slaughtered them. The existence of this major tradition in my upbringing probably did the least to prepare me for my long term vegan life. I have been a grateful vegan for 20 years. I am grateful for my good health at nearly age 50, as well as for my lifelong vegan, very well developed, highly intelligent, and healthy daughter. I am grateful for the peace of mind I have; being aware that we can live and let live peacefully with our fellow animals. I will be vegan forever because once we find Peace, nothing else will do.

Once we have learned to heal, there is no room to kill. Once we know we can tread on the Earth lightly, leaving room for those with whom we share this magnificent planet, including our fellow animals, there is no other way but being a vegan. I love life, and so do all our fellow sentient beings. How could I possibly ever decide that they are mere commodities to be used as things? Once we awaken to the Vegan Truth, there is no turning back. Veganism is an ethic; a lifesaving ethic.

I will be a vegan forever because this is the least I can do for our fellow sentient beings. I will be a vegan forever because right is right. We human animals are simply one kind of animal among many others. I forgave myself that as a child I was following traditions blindly versus making my own choices. I know better now. I know I can live, and let live. I am gratefully aware that veganism is a joy, not a sacrifice! I know I am an abolitionist vegan for life...for ALL lives.

It is my calling to advocate for non-human animal rights; also known as veganism. I encourage you to consider becoming vegan, and save innocent lives with us!

Janine Laura Bronson, Israel/United Kingdom/USA

I pray that the vegan way will become the norm, and we vegans shall no longer be part of a minority. When I think "vegan" I remember, with gratitude in my heart, the late fellow-Brit, Donald Watson, of blessed memory, who coined the term.

I was born in London, England, and have been vegan most of my life, and for dozens of years have been following the compassionate lifestyle of a Kosher-Raw-Living-Foods-Ethical-Ecological-Vegan; mostly organic, and local (growing vegetables and fruit trees in California, which is my home now). Nothing is more rewarding, when considering the kinds of nourishment one can obtain, than munching on fresh produce, picked freshly from your own garden. However, veganism is not just a diet to satisfy ones culinary desires. For example, we also should not wear clothing made from animal products, and I'm happy to say that there is now an alternative to wearing standard (Jewish) Tefillin (phylacteries) that is vegan (non-leather).

As a vegan, I see a parallel between peace and veganism, which is why I joined several events at the Jerusalem Peace Making Tours. There is a growing trend to make Israel a vegan country by law! *Kashrut* is a road-map to veganism because of the commandment to not cause pain and suffering to any creature, not just humans. A member of the Israeli political governing party, Mordechai Ben-Porat, introduced a bill to the Knesset (equivalent to Congress in the US), to make it illegal to eat any flesh from an animal! Even if that law has not yet passed, there will come a time when living vegan will become a more popular lifestyle, and vegans will be the majority, not only in Israel, but all over the "ever-more-peaceful" world, Amen.

Photo by Hof Butenland farmed animal sanctuary, Germany

Jenna Fox, Bristol, United Kingdom

Veganism is about respect for others, treating them fairly and as you would like to be treated, and extending this consideration to include non-human animals. Animals have been excluded for being members of a different species to our own, and treated as property and resources. However, like us, animals are sentient beings who wish to avoid suffering and harm.

Increasingly it is recognised as unjust to treat others badly merely because they are different from us. Efforts are being made to eliminate forms of discrimination such as racism, sexism, heterosexism, etc. and the resulting harms they cause. When it comes to animals, we have all been brought up entrenched in another form of discrimination that we are largely unaware of, known as "speciesism"; where animals become the objectified "other".

While many already empathise with favoured non-humans and would object to harming them, most people unthinkingly consume animal products every day without giving a second thought to the harm this causes the animals used in the process.

My wakeup call came when I saw a video depicting caged cats and dogs in Asia waiting to be killed and eaten. I saw this as monstrous and wondered how anyone could do such a thing. In the next scene chickens were being slaughtered. I realised that there was no difference between doing it to one animal or another. They were all the same. Nobody wants to die! There is no acceptable way to exploit or kill someone.

Once one recognises animals as individuals with personalities, feelings and the capacity to suffer, one can empathise with all of them. Vegans are those who see that it is not just humans or any particular favoured species who are sentient persons worthy of respect. All conscious beings are deserving of moral consideration, including the ones we use for food, fashion, experimentation, entertainment, etc. If it is not acceptable to exploit or harm a child or a dog, then it is not acceptable to do so to any animal.

I will always be vegan, because animals are persons and a person is someone to respect, not something to use.

Gabija Enciūtė, Vilnius, Lithuania

Am I going to stay vegan all my life?

In 2010, a group of neuroscientists from the Cuban Neuroscience Center published the results of their research under the title, *The Brain Functional Networks Associated to Human and Animal Suffering Differ among Omnivores, Vegetarians and Vegans*. The scientists involved explained the main question posed: "We hypothesized that vegetarians and vegans, who made their feeding choice for ethical reasons, might show brain responses to conditions of suffering involving humans or animals."

The main experiment in the study was conducted thus: in groups matched for sex and age, participants were alternately shown pictures of natural landscapes and violent pictures with humans and animals that were murdered, mutilated, tortured, wounded, etc. Their brain activation was investigated using fMRI. Substantial differences were found, not only between vegetarians/vegans and omnivores, but also between vegans and vegetarians. The study concludes that empathy towards members of different species "has different neural representation among individuals with different feeding habits, perhaps reflecting different motivational factors and beliefs." This essentially means that our eating and lifestyle habits—or, more likely, our realisation that motivates us and leads us to choose those habits—leaves an imprint in our brain.

The study by the Cuban Neuroscience Center proves that most of the empathy-related processes in the vegan respondents' brains happen mainly in the cortex, which is the newest (and the most evolutionary-advanced) part of the human brain. Apparently, the workings of certain parts of the cortex provide vegans with more sophisticated contextual thinking and with the ability to evaluate the consequences of their actions better.

I would like to think of this change in the brain as a little step in human evolution. If it really is so, it should be strange to even ask oneself whether one is going to remain vegan all one's life. Nature went so far as to provide my brain with the only sensible change that could possibly have a positive effect on the life of the planet. It will definitely make sure that this little experiment continues.

Ireene Viktor, Estonia

It´s actually quite simple—I will always be vegan because it´s the right thing to do. It´s not necessary to use animals and eat animals or animal products nor is it morally justified.

Veganism is not about one´s personal health or well-being. Of course vegans should eat healthy, and a plant-based diet is very healthy, but this should not be the sole purpose of ditching animal products. And it´s not only about compassion to animals either. You don´t have to be an animal lover to be a vegan. I am not. Yes, animals are cute and all that, but we should just leave them be, where necessary help them but otherwise just let them live their own lives, not use them, not exploit them, not kill them.

It´s about making the connection and realizing that your actions and your choices make a difference, and that you are directly responsible for killing thousands of innocent beings, and contribute to the suffering of many more. For me it´s about non-violence. Imagine a world where all forms of violence are looked upon as extreme. Sadly, today we live in a world where violence is considered normal and natural. We might think that Western society has almost abolished violence, that we live in a liberal society where lives matter and where equality is seen as a basic right. Well, think again, open your eyes and go vegan! It will be the best decision of your life!

Photo provided by Karrel Christopher - www.karrelchristopher.com

Mel Weinstein, Decatur, Illinois, USA

I have been on a vegan path for 8 years and will continue to my final day. I will always be a vegan, because I cannot return to the attitudes and behaviors of my earlier life.

Once I learned about the egregious suffering and short lives of farmed animals raised as food in our culture, there was no turning back. Once I learned about the abusive practices common in the leather, wool, silk, fur, entertainment, and cosmetics industries, there was no turning back. Once I learned that animals have feelings, emotions, and personalities, just like me, there was no turning back. Once I looked deeply into the eyes of my companion animals and asked myself why I looked upon them with favor, but ignored the millions of exploited animals in our society, there was no turning back. Once I understood that what I ate, what I wore, and how I entertained myself, had consequences for animals, there was no turning back.

Once I realized that the spiritual practices that I embraced, such as Ahimsa, centered on reverence for life, not just mine or other humans, but all beings, there was no turning back. Once I became more aware of the connection between the livestock industry and the devastation of rainforests and other ecosystems, including valuable water supplies, there was no turning back. Once I gained a realization that a plant-based diet was far superior to a meat-based one for health, well-being, and longevity, there was no turning back.

Even though there is no such thing as a perfect vegan lifestyle, I know, both in my heart and mind, there is a perfect vegan mindset that cultivates an attitude of respect and reverence towards all living beings, and, because of that perspective, I will always be a vegan!

120

Scott Wilson, Melbourne, Australia

For me, spirituality is a big thing. Michael Lerner has great description of what is spiritual: ethics, aesthetics, love, compassion, creativity, music, altruism, generosity, forgiveness, spontaneity, emergent phenomena, consciousness itself, and any other aspect of reality not subject to empirical verification or measurement. So for me to believe I am a spiritual person and commit cruelty, or to indirectly support cruelty, would be terrible on any level. I cannot reconcile eating, wearing or consuming sentient beings; holding fast to the ethic of "equal consideration of interests". Since my ethics are tightly woven into my spirituality, I could never consider harming any living being intentionally.

Also, consumerism and corporate greed disgust me. To participate in or support such a cruel and unethical system would be unthinkable. I have children and feel very obligated to living a life they are proud of. They will have children and what type of legacy am I leaving, and what type of planet are they going to be living on? Considering the current state of things, it's not looking good. I believe in the power of the people; if enough of us protest and boycott stuff that is causing harm, we will change the world.

This vegan lifestyle is not easy and can cause some friends to part company; even family members. Still, if we remain indifferent as some may choose, we are on the side of the oppressors. I refuse to choose indifference and I am proud to be vegan. The gains far outweigh the losses. Real change takes commitment and sacrifice; it's costly. For me the price is small in comparison to the barbaric practices. The biblical story David and Goliath comes to mind. Great metaphor for the struggle vegans face; a struggle I am convinced is already changing the world as people are starting to notice us.

Finally, for me it would be unthinkable to live any other way. What a great planet it would be if the whole world switched to a vegan lifestyle. Non-vegans would say I have utopian, idealist thoughts. I would say they have unsustainable, cruel, meaningless ideas. Intelligence, spirituality and good ethics should prevail. According to all the science, man has evolved. We should not be taking steps backwards by encouraging industrial farming—we should be evolving forward into more caring, loving human beings.

Munjeeta Sohal, Busan, South Korea

Born in the United Kingdom and now living in South Korea

I will always be vegan because I have come to the realization that making "humane choices" as a consumer isn't the point. What we should be concerned about is the fact that the animals that are killed or used at all. It took me some time to get here, but now that I have, I can't imagine going back.

Eating a plant-based diet and avoiding buying products which are made from or tested on animals just makes sense, morally and environmentally. It means living a day to day life that is more compassionate and mindful; making the choice has made me a better, more thoughtful person in everything I do. For profit to take priority over morals makes me sick to my stomach: the fact that meat is a commodity and produced as cheaply as possible to satisfy the ever-growing demand for it at the expense of caring for animals. Being unable to access transparent animal welfare legislation has made me suspicious of how laws are made and enforced. Then there is the myriad of reasons relating to health and the environment that explain why I will always be vegan.

Seeing videos of humans mistreating animals, which we then eat, wear and use as entertainment—like objects—means I will never buy another animal product as long as I live. Watching chickens being stamped on, pigs being sworn at and hit with metal bars, cows dangling by one leg and struggling while their throats are slit makes me too scared that the animal I am eating or wearing suffered. Watching cows running after their calves as they are taken away soon after they are born, and seeing hens with no feathers and sores from metal egg-laying cages, means I will never let dairy products or eggs pass my lips again.

And, even if animals are treated humanely, what gives humans the right to exploit them? Why should my desire to eat an egg override a hen's natural instinct to nest and rear a chick? Even if a cow lives a happy life, do I have the right to slaughter the cow for its skin before its natural lifespan is up? I believe not, and this is why I will always be a vegan.

Ultimately though, I will always be a vegan because I simply do not need to eat or wear animals to be healthy and happy. Plant-based eating has opened up a whole world of flavor and compassion that I would never have known existed if I hadn't become vegan.

Chelsea Dub, Indiana, USA

Designer of back cover illustration

I will always be vegan because as an autistic person and neurodiversity advocate, I refuse to deny other animals the dignity I demand for autistic and other neurodivergent humans. Neurodiversity—acknowledging and respecting differences in neurology—should include all beings. Both autistic people and non-human animals are affected by the same ableism that considers our brains to be deficient and invalidates our experiences and existences. The school bully who torments an autistic student for being a "retard" is applying the same prejudice at dinnertime when they mock the suffering of chickens because they are "just stupid animals". This is where ableism and speciesism overlap.

Because autistics do not always express ourselves in normalized ways, we are perceived to be robotic and lacking in empathy which perpetuates the discrimination and abuse of autistic people. Non-humans are considered to be emotionless and more like machines than sentient beings and are used as production units, transportation devices, entertainment systems, and experimental models. Society also correlates sentience and intelligence with speaking ability, and so nonverbal autistics and non-human animals are assumed to be unfeeling or unthinking.

One of the earliest memories I have is from when I was speech delayed (an autism trait) and was unable to tell my parents about an abusive daycare. Through tears, I struggled to convert the words in my head into speech. Thankfully, my mom sensed that something was wrong, and my parents pulled me out of that daycare immediately. Although I was not speaking, I was communicating, and it is important to distinguish the two because speech is just one form of communication. Unfortunately, speech is privileged over other forms of communication, which strips nonverbal individuals of their agency. However, just as I communicated without words to my parents so many years ago, a cow bellowing for her kidnapped calf and a pig squealing in a slaughterhouse are clearly communicating their distress without needing to verbalize it. It is important in animal advocacy to remember that we are not "voices for the voiceless", but are amplifying voices that have been ignored and silenced. Similarly, it is crucial in autistic advocacy for neurotypicals to consider the voices of autistics, whether they are expressed through speech, text, sign language, or other forms of augmentative and alternative communication. Neurodiversity means embracing different minds, and my mind is neither inferior nor superior to anyone else's, which is why I will always be vegan.

Final Words

Compiling these essays was truly fun. It was wonderful to speak with vegans around the world, since at one time I was the only vegan I knew.

This book is not asking you to take baby steps in the direction of becoming vegan. It is not an attempt to lure you toward doing the right thing by telling you that your own health will benefit if you do. This book's purpose is to explore and express the true meaning of veganism, and to inspire its readers to join this rapidly growing social justice movement taking root all over the globe.

Becoming vegan allows us to live the truth that we already know inside ourselves; since we humans are able to live our lives without causing intentional harm to others, this means that we do not have the right to exploit, objectify, enslave, assault, or kill any other sentient beings. Please join us in our effort to change the world, for the better.

For more information about the vegan way of life, please visit www.gentleworld.org.

~ M 'Butterflies' Katz

Photo by El Hogar ProVegan animal sanctuary, Spain - www.elhogarprovegan.org

The above quote is from a song entitled 'We'll keep marching 'til they're all free' written by Light (co-founder of Gentle World) for the June 1990 *March for The Animals* in Washington, D.C.

Why I will ALWAYS be vegan; 125 essays from around the world
~ first edition, published July, 2015

Made in the USA
Middletown, DE
18 March 2017